Making the
Hours Count

Transforming Your **Service** Experience

Student Book

Making the
Hours Count

Transforming Your **Service** Experience

Student Book

Constance Fourré

Saint Mary's Press®

Genuine recycled paper with 10% post-consumer waste. 5111900

The publishing team included Steven C. McGlaun, development editor; Lorraine Kilmartin, reviewer; Mary Koehler, permissions editor; manufacturing coordinated by the prepress and production services departments of Saint Mary's Press.

Printed in the United States of America

Printing: 9 8 7 6 5 4 3 2 1

Year: 2014 13 12 11 10 09 08 07 06

ISBN-13: 978-0-88489-917-4
ISBN-10: 0-88489-917-9

Library of Congress Cataloging-in-Publication Data
Fourré, Constance.
Making the hours count : transforming your service experience. Student book / Constance Fourré.
     p. cm.
ISBN-13: 978-0-88489-917-4 (spiral)
ISBN-10: 0-88489-917-9 (spiral)
     1. Catholic youth—Religious life. 2. Youth in church work. 3. Student service. I. Title.
BX2355.F68 2006
248.8'3088282—dc22

                                                                2005033257

This book is dedicated to two groups of people. First, to the many in our Church and in our world who give their lives every day in service to those who are marginalized. Their generosity, courage, wisdom, and joy provide light for us all. Second, to the young members of our Church who will someday take their place and be inspired by their example. May these pages help create the bridge between the two.

I would like to thank the members of the Benilde–Saint Margaret's School community who have worked so faithfully in the field of service, especially Susan Cipolle, Lisa Lenhart-Murphy, Paul Freid, and Zach Zeckser. With the staunch support of our administration, they have nurtured a desire for service and a hunger for justice among our students for many years.

I would also like to thank my editor, Steven McGlaun, who developed the concept for this book and championed it to its completion. Steven provided a perfect balance of encouragement and judicious feedback, and his good nature and good humor were unfailing. Such wise and warm support is a precious resource.

Contents

Introduction

The Transforming Power of Service

Welcome! You are about to begin a wonderful adventure. You are starting a project that has the potential to change your life forever. Service has helped young people choose a career, strengthen traits like kindness and generosity, and develop skills that can strengthen relationships. Service can bring you fun, laughter, and cherished memories.

You may be a rookie, venturing for the first time into the world of service. Perhaps you are a veteran, returning to a familiar project or tackling something new, expanding your horizons even further. Wherever you are, this book can help. The first four chapters give practical guidance on finding the right spot for you and getting off to the best start possible. Rookies may need this information more than veterans, although every volunteer experience is unique.

Chapters five through nine are quite different. They are designed to help you see service and justice more deeply, to transform your service, and to help it transform you. Getting to know new people and helping them and yourself through service are great opportunities. But there can be more.

Think back to your first days in junior high. You were probably excited, scared, and a little bewildered when you arrived. You knew you were making a new start, entering a new era in your life. But now, as you look back on those days, you realize just how much your life has changed. You did not understand at that time all the dimensions of growing up.

You're older now, and you may have a fair idea of what you're about with this project. But there are dimensions you probably don't yet see. Service isn't just helping people in need. It also has the potential to influence the person you become. Reflecting on your experience and working through some of the information in this book can help you understand the world, your own values, and yourself on a far deeper level. Reflection combined with experience is powerful.

These pages are designed to help you look beyond the faces of the people you will see—important as they are. You will gain insight into the experiences that influence people whose lives are different from yours, and you will discover why some inequalities exist. You will get a chance to reflect on short-term and long-term solutions to issues, and how you can be part of either. You will get guidance and experience in solving problems and handling conflict creatively. You will have a chance to reflect on how being Catholic can help form your ideals and anchor your place in the world.

Athletes determine their performance in the pool or on the field each day in their practice sessions. In the same way, the decisions you make as a young person influence the kind of adult you will become. You get to decide whether you will be an active citizen or someone who just sits back and lets things happen. Thoughtful service can help you discover the path to being a person who makes a difference.

And, through your project, you may receive a smile from someone whose day would have been bleak without your presence; feel the victory of a disabled child who smacks her first baseball; have the satisfaction of seeing a tidy, freshly painted house where before there was peeling paint and a weedy lawn; or provide your city council with new information that prompts them to protect an endangered wetland. Those achievements are priceless.

How to Use This Book

If you are using this book as part of a class, your teacher will direct you through the book. If you are serving on your own, here are a few suggestions.

First, glance over chapters one through four. Find your own starting point and begin working your way through the process of setting up your project and getting started. Look over chapters eight and nine, on analysis and advocacy, before selecting your project.

After you've begun your project, take a look at chapters five through nine. These chapters have a lot of information. It would be hard to read them through in one sitting. A better approach is to read sections over the course of your project, applying them one piece at a time.

You don't need to read these chapters in order. You may want to go back over some sections as your work progresses. The last chapter helps you evaluate your experience and gather wisdom before moving on. If you choose your project wisely and invest yourself in it, you will be amazed at what will fill those pages.

Time to Get Started

As you start your service experience, don't shy away from being daring. As the title of this book states, make the hours count. With an open heart, service is more than meeting a predetermined amount of hours. It has the power to transform the world and you.

Chapter 1
You and Your Project

Finding the Right Match

You're ready to begin the process of finding your service project. This chapter will help you examine the hopes, gifts, experience, and concerns you bring to your service work. It will help you begin to narrow down your choices and form a clearer picture of the joys and challenges of the next months.

A service project's success depends a lot on finding the right match. Plenty of great service opportunities are out there, but not all of them would be great for you. By taking some time now to assess your own strengths and interests you increase the chances of having a happier and more successful service experience. You bring a lot to this venture. You have talents and gifts, your own personal style, experience, and curiosity about the world you have yet to discover. You may take some of your talents and skills for granted—or there may be some you have not yet discovered.

The inventories that follow are designed to help you take a look at yourself, your experiences, your preferences, and some of your goals. They can help you identify what you bring to your service work and the areas where you would like to grow. They provide a foundation for the next chapter, when you will decide on the specific service project you will take on.

Your Personal Style

This first inventory takes a look at your personal style. Each person has preferences that influence how he or she behaves in most situations. For example, some people enjoy both working alone and spending time in large groups. Others get bored and restless when they're alone, while still others feel anxious or tired when they're with large groups of people they don't know. Each personality style has its own gifts to contribute. The trick is to match the right personality to the right job, if possible.

Personality Style

Place a check mark in front of the statements that best describe you. It is okay to check two contradictory statements.

____   I like to meet new people—the more the better.

____   I like to have long-term relationships with a few people.

____   I enjoy the challenge of the unexpected.

____   I am more comfortable when things are predictable.

____   I like to know what's expected of me.

____   I like to figure out what needs to be done and do it.

____   I'm comfortable telling people what to do.

____   I prefer to have someone else in charge.

____   I am good at thinking on my feet.

____   I enjoy meeting people who are different from myself.

____   I am a practical person.

____   I enjoy working by myself.

____   I like being with small groups of people.

____   I'm good at organizing things.

____   I would prefer to have one service project and stick with it.

____   I would prefer to try a variety of different service projects.

____   I'm comfortable being with people who are in pain.

____   I do well working under pressure.

____   I like to get a project completed.

____   I like open-ended projects.

____   I like to listen.

____   I like to talk.

The People You've Met

Put an X in front of people you've known.
Put an O in front of people you'd be interested in getting to know.

X	O	
____	____	elderly people
____	____	children with mental disabilities
____	____	children with physical disabilities

___ ___ adults with mental disabilities
___ ___ adults with physical disabilities
___ ___ people who are sick or injured
___ ___ preschoolers
___ ___ elementary school–age children
___ ___ middle school students
___ ___ people who come from another culture
___ ___ people who are active in making a difference

Stepping Outside of Your Comfort Zone

Your personal style inventory will help you select a project that is comfortable for you. While feeling at ease is important, stretching your comfort zone is also valuable. For example, a student named Laura was persuaded by a friend to volunteer in a nursing home. Laura had very little experience with elderly people and wasn't sure how they would behave or how she would respond. She was terrified before her first day and made her friend promise not to leave her side.

On that first day Laura discovered she had an exceptional ability to connect with the elderly. She was so thrilled that the following day she raced down the hall to find me and share her good news. Before long she was working with Alzheimer's patients, loving the residents no matter how confused or even angry they became. A staff member told her, "Everybody is somebody's child." Laura learned that this adage applied to everyone, whether they were nine or ninety, and this belief stayed with her long after she left her volunteer position. Laura took a chance that she could get comfortable in a new setting, and it paid off. As you select a project, consider signing up for work that would expand your comfort zone. You may discover new strengths and talents in yourself that would never have emerged if you'd chosen to stay only in familiar territory.

> "You are ready for what Christ wants of you now. He wants you—all of you—to be the light of the world, as only young people can be light. It is time to let your light shine!"
>
> (Pope John Paul II, January 26, 1999)

Your Interests and Skills

You carry your personal style with you wherever you go and in everything you do. You've developed specific interests and skills you can share with someone else. You don't have to be exceptional in any of these areas to be able to share them effectively. The following inventory will help you call to mind abilities you have that could be valuable to someone else. It can also help you see what kind of project you would be interested in choosing.

Place an X in front of your skills and interests.

____   Athletics

   Which sports?

____   Music

   Which instrument(s)?

   Voice

____   Theater

____   Academics

   Your best subjects:

   Your worst subjects:

____   Politics

____   Recreation

____   The outdoors

____   Animals

____   Your faith

____   Exercise

____   Computers

____   Other

Your Past Experience

You may have experiences outside of school or extracurricular activities that provide you with valuable skills or insight in selecting a project. Take a few minutes to write down any pertinent experience we haven't yet mentioned and to consider what you may have learned from that experience.

I have the following paid or unpaid experience:
(Examples: babysitting, coaching T-ball, teaching Sunday school, working in an office, and so on)

What I have learned about myself from this experience:
(For example: I have patience, I'm not good at taking charge, I can stand up to pressure, and so on.)

Areas in which I'd like to grow:
(Try to pick three areas where you would like to improve.)

Can I Make a Difference?

You may wonder whether the work you are about to do is really important. Sometimes when we look at all the problems in the world we can start to feel hopeless. As you begin your project you may feel overwhelmed. You see children who are abused, or newcomers to our country who have lost their homelands, and you realize hundreds of thousands of people are like them. On some days it seems as though we're trying to empty the ocean with a bucket. In later chapters we will explore the many ways your service project can make a difference in your life and for those you serve.

Myth or Reality?

One definition of *myth* is, "a traditional story of supposedly historical events that serves to unfold part of the world's view of a people or explain a practice, belief, or natural phenomenon." Although *myth* can have more than one meaning, in this book we will be talking about myths as inaccurate assumptions we may carry into our projects. Reality, on the other hand, is people and situations as they truly exist. Having a realistic view of our experience is being able to see not only circumstances or people's behaviors but also to understand why they occur.

One potential benefit of service for us can be the opportunity to develop a more accurate picture of our world. We develop beliefs and assumptions about people and our world based on the media, what we hear from those around us, and from our experience. Sometimes our beliefs are accurate; often they are biased or just incomplete—in other words, we accept myths because we don't have enough information or experience to judge more correctly.

An assumption is a belief we develop without really checking it out. Unexamined assumptions can limit our ability to experience the world as it really is. For example, one hundred years ago most people in the United States assumed that women were not as intelligent as men and were very limited physically. Few people challenged that assumption because it never occurred to them there was any other way to think. Most women would not even consider running competitively, for example, because they assumed they did not have the physical stamina to run long distances. Because they exercised so little, if they had tried to run a mile their false assumption would have been confirmed. Women lost opportunities and joys we take for granted today because it did not occur to them or those around them that they could have more.

You may well have inaccurate assumptions about the people you are about to serve and the places you will go. These assumptions are simply the result of lack of experience. In this book we will take a look at assumptions that may get in your way or the way of people around you. These assumptions may affect how you treat certain people, how you vote, where you choose to live, and the people you allow into your life. Discovering that some of our beliefs are incorrect can help us become a little more open and curious as we go into new situations. In the future you may be able to share what you have learned with other people who have not had your opportunities.

How Christian Service Is Different

Public schools across the country have developed strong programs that give millions of students a chance to serve. But this program is different. You are taking on this project as a member of a parish or as a student at a Catholic school. Your program has a faith dimension that is not necessarily a part of other people's service efforts, no matter how generous they may be.

In a later chapter we will talk about Catholic social teaching, the Church's Tradition on how we should handle ourselves in a complex, interrelated world. For now, we will talk about what it means to serve as a Christian.

On Being a Believer

Christians don't necessarily serve any more generously or more skillfully than others. People who believe in God or a higher power don't necessarily behave better than nonbelievers, but faith does add an extra dimension to our work.

The difference might be compared to owning a bicycle. You might have a bicycle you love: it is designed for the riding you do, you like the way the bike looks, it is lightweight and portable. If the bicycle was also a final gift from a beloved grandfather who has since passed away, it takes on an added dimension. You value the bike not only for what it is and can do but also because it represents the kindness and generosity of the grandfather who bestowed it. The bike is a symbol and reminder of who your grandfather is for you.

People who engage well in service see the people they serve as important and unique. If we believe in a loving God, we also see those people as children of God. Each person is precious, regardless of how he or she looks or behaves, because God created everyone. God put them in the world for a reason. Even a child who is utterly helpless because of developmental or physical disabilities is precious in God's eyes and in our eyes as well.

On Being a Christian

What does it mean to you to be a Christian? Sometimes people equate being a Christian with being nice, as in, "That wasn't a very Christian thing to do." What we usually mean is, "That wasn't a very kind or ethical thing to do." Being a Christian has a more precise meaning; after all, people of other faiths are called to be kind and ethical, too.

To be a Christian means to be a follower of Jesus. Some people follow Jesus much as others follow Mahatma Gandhi: they consider Jesus to be a great teacher and role model, but they do not consider him to be the Son of God. You may find yourself in this category. Others follow Jesus not only because his message inspires but also because we believe he is God's Son. We not only use his words and example as a model, we believe Jesus is present in us and in those we meet.

Some people believe in Jesus, but their beliefs don't make a practical difference in their lives. If we truly are doing Christian service, our work will be affected in two primary ways: finding guidance and strength from God, and seeing God in the people we serve.

Seeing God in Others

Some people seem to easily see God in others. This is not necessarily because their faith is stronger. Some extroverts see Jesus readily in the face of others, and more introverted people may need quiet time alone to connect with God and then see God in their relationships.

A service experience is a way of stepping into a relationship with God. That may come about because you meet someone who has suffered tremendously but whose faith shines through a joyful demeanor. It may be because we are humbled by the suffering of a child and we need to turn to God to find meaning. It may happen because our hearts are opened by the work we do, and when we open our hearts we discover God is there.

"But I'm Not Sure . . ."

Adolescence is a time of questioning. Many readers of this book may be unsure about their faith. Some may not have grown up with a very strong faith. Others may have had a strong child's faith but are in the process of reworking and moving toward a more adult relationship with God.

Doubts and questions aren't bad, and they don't mean we can't operate from a Christian perspective. Doubts in a relationship with God are much like questions we have in a relationship with another human, whether a parent, a friend, a boyfriend, or a girlfriend. Having questions doesn't mean you are not in a relationship. It simply means you are reflecting on your relationship. Growth in faith can happen in many ways. You don't need to be sure as you start this project; you only need to be open.

Looking Ahead

You are probably having a lot of thoughts and emotions as you look ahead to your project. Most people who have done service, especially for the first time, say that their project turned out to be much different than they had anticipated. They learned things they'd never hoped to learn, discovered things about themselves that they hadn't dreamed.

Expectations of Yourself

Take a few moments to write your expectations of yourself when you have finished your project. Give the expectations to a teacher or staff person, or set it aside to be read again in a few months. It will be interesting to compare the reality with your expectations. Use the questions below to help you envision your expectations.

- What type of service work do you envision for yourself?

(Remember, you haven't yet made a commitment. This may change.)

- What strengths will you bring to your service?
- What part(s) of yourself will be challenged during your service?
- How will your experience change you?
- What will you like most about service?
- What are your fears?
- At the end of your work, how do you think you will feel overall about your experience?

Prayer

O Lord, you have searched me and known me.
You know when I sit down and when I rise up;
> You discern my thoughts from far away.
You search out my path and my lying down,
> and are acquainted with all my ways.
Even before a word is on my tongue,
> O Lord, you know it completely.

. . . .

For it was you who formed my inward parts;
> You knit me together in my mother's womb.

(Psalm 139:1–4,13)

Take some quiet time. Read this passage from Psalm 139, and imagine yourself as you begin your service project. Close with this or another prayer:

God,
Thank you for the opportunity that lies before me. You know I'm feeling uncertain about where to go and how my service will turn out. Please open my heart as I choose my project, and guide me to the place that will best use my gifts. Help me find the resources I need to make a wise choice and do a good job. Thank you for your constant love and guidance.
Amen.

Chapter 2
MAKING THE CONNECTION

Where Will You Go?

In the last chapter we began to clarify some of the qualities, skills, and experiences you bring to your service project and what you hope to gain. Now it's time to get down to the practical matter of selecting a specific project. You may be doing service hours for Confirmation, as a requirement for graduation, or simply volunteering on your own. If you are working with a service coordinator, don't forget to rely on her or him for guidance to get you started. However, even if your school or parish service program is well established, you may have an interest that it does not address.

On the other hand, you may be working without a lot of outside guidance and support. In that case, the following information may be especially helpful. In chapter 1 you got a general idea of your interests. Moving to the next step, finding the best project for you, is critical to the quality of the experience you will have in your project. For example, the service coordinator at the school where I teach has done a wide range of service work over the years. She enjoyed a variety of challenges, from working with gang members to taking students on wilderness experiences. She likes to stretch herself mentally and physically. But the time she signed up to teach a cooking class was beyond her. Even though the project was "easier," it was just not a good match for her. She was exhausted by the end of the class, and never got to the point where she felt she was successful. It's not a question of whether a project is "hard" or "easy," it's a question of whether it is right for you.

You may make your selection by looking at the people you will work with, or an issue you will focus on. For example, you may have a particular concern for unwanted animals or the environment or pro-life issues. You would be happy in a range of activities, as long as they pertain to your special interest. Or you may enjoy a certain activity, such as skiing, and the way you use that skill is flexible.

Revisiting the Personal Inventories

Take a look at the inventories you filled out in chapter 1. Using them as a guide, answer the following questions.

- Are certain issues important to you? Would you like to learn more about them? If so, list up to three of them below:

- Would you like to work with certain groups of people, such as the elderly, immigrants, or little kids? Are there any groups you know you would prefer not to work with?

- What skills and interests do you bring that might be a match for the people or issues you have listed?

- What abilities would you most like to use with this project? Remember to use the checklists from the previous chapter to help you decide.

Think creatively—don't let yourself be limited to the obvious. For example, one student taught exercise classes to nursing home residents who were confined to wheelchairs. Some art students created a mural to brighten the walls of a youth group room. Special Olympics volunteers coached athletes with developmental disabilities. Another student used his computer skills to create and maintain a Web site for a child protection agency.

Stretching Yourself

Keep in mind what was said earlier about being willing to stretch beyond your comfort zone. Just because you don't have experience with a group of people doesn't mean you wouldn't be good with them and enjoy working with them. You may not yet have the skills to begin a conversation with an elderly person or find common ground with a preschooler. But your sense of humor, curiosity, warmth, or ability to play may be just what is needed to draw someone out and create a welcoming atmosphere. There are some wonderful people out there just waiting for you to meet them.

When you visit an agency, you may see staff and volunteers who seem totally at ease—experts in making connections. If you talk to them, you will discover they started out just as you are today—unsure and wondering if they could be successful. Many people discover their career through a volunteer experience. And many of them were surprised at first to discover they could feel at home in their new environment.

Finding What's Already There

Once you have a general idea of what you would like to do, you need to decide where you will do it. Sometimes volunteers waste a lot of energy trying to create a project from scratch. There may be a perfectly good agency out there doing work that interests you. An agency is any organized group, such as a school, a nursing home, a hospital, a shelter, an advocacy group, and so on. If you don't take the time to check out already existing organizations, you may lose a lot of time and make mistakes trying to come up with a solution on your own. You might even miss out altogether because you don't know how to connect with the people you're interested in serving.

It's worthwhile to check out existing organizations in your community. Your program coordinator, if you have one, is the first person to ask about this. But don't stop there. Below you will find several ways you can begin searching for your service opportunity.

Hotlines and Directories

In larger communities, a hotline or directory of services lists addresses and phone numbers for agencies. The United Way, for example, is a large organization that publishes directories called *First Call for Help*. The directory is a thorough listing of agencies that provide a broad range of services, and many communities have them. Your school or parish may have a hard copy of the directory, or you can access it online.

The Yellow Pages

The yellow pages of your telephone directory are also a good resource. Check under headings like shelters, nursing homes, schools, hospitals, senior citizens, social service agencies, museums, animal shelters, AIDS information and treatment, crisis intervention, athletic organizations. Look for the yellow pages index, which will give a listing of topics and where to look for them.

An Internet Search

Try an Internet search by keying in the type of work you would like to do and the name of your city or town. Or simply type in a topic that interests or concerns you. There are national and international efforts, such as Free the Children or Habitat for Humanity that you can join. Catholic Charities, the Church's largest relief organization, has great information on their Web site. If you live in a rural area or a small town, you may need to look beyond your borders to find a project that interests you. You may even want to travel to take part in a project such as Habitat for Humanity.

Parish Connections

Your parish is a wonderful resource. Parishioners or staff members who are involved in service may be glad to include you. Or you might want to volunteer in your parish in the nursery, the choir, as an usher or lector, in the religious education or youth program, or in the parish school. Also, don't overlook your youth minister as a resource in helping you find a service experience.

Your Neighborhood

Pay attention to your neighborhood. Is there an interesting organization located near you, or do you pass near an agency on your way to work, school, or games?

Ask your family and friends. Maybe your parents know someone who's involved in a cause, or your aunts or uncles could have a special interest you might share. A friend may already be involved in a project; he or she can give you company and support on those first important sessions.

The Guidance of a Mentor

Especially if you don't have a service coordinator to work with, finding a trusted adult to act as a mentor for you can be tremendously helpful. A mentor can give you suggestions and encourage you if you get discouraged. She or he can help you troubleshoot, and let you know if a challenge you encounter is "normal" or something that should give you second thoughts about a project. Ask a parent, teacher, youth group leader, or other adult if she or he would be willing to coach you through this process. She or he will probably be pleased to be asked.

Designing a New Project

Perhaps you can't find an organization to help you. You may have an interest that other people haven't thought of, or you may have a new solution to a problem that's been around forever. Don't let yourself be limited only to solutions already available.

Look around your community for things needing change or people who aren't being served. Perhaps a nearby playground has unsafe equipment or surfacing. Maybe an intersection needs a traffic light. There may be a polluted lake or stream nearby. A disabled child in your neighborhood may be lonely. Elementary-age students near you may be unsupervised after school.

What are some needs you've observed that you, alone or with a group of people, might help fill?

Books Can Help

The Kids' Guide to Service Projects, by Barbara Lewis (Minneapolis: Free Spirit Publishing, 1996), is probably the best resource to help you really tailor a project to your interests and strengths. Marc and Craig Kielburger's book *Take Action: A Guide to Active Citizenship* (Hoboken, NJ: Wiley & Sons, Inc., 2002) is also good. Here are just a few examples you may not have thought of:

- clean up a vacant lot
- work for voter registration
- organize a project to buy and install locks and smoke alarms for seniors
- create a play that teaches children about being safe after school
- sponsor a recycling contest at your school

Making the Contact

The next few pages will help you connect with an agency. Even if you think you will be working on your own, you may get some good ideas for recruiting help for your project from these tips and suggestions.

Phone Tips

If you have found an agency you would like to work with, your first step is to contact it. This may be tougher than it seems. It can be hard to pick up the phone and call someone you don't know, especially if this is your first experience. Just remember—you have something to offer that the agency needs. Most agencies are delighted to hear from young people willing to help. Unfortunately, that doesn't mean the connection will be easy.

It is not uncommon for agencies to be short on staff. They often run on very tight budgets, and so the volunteer coordinator (if they have one) may be very busy and often not at his or her desk. You may call several times and never get an answer. At the same time, the agency may have trouble finding you. Students spend a lot of time away from a phone: in class, practicing or competing in sports, or in an activity.

Learn to take care of business via voice mail. This is a skill you will find useful in other parts of your life. If a receptionist answers the phone and the person you need to speak to is not in, ask to be put through to voice mail. Leave a message on voice mail or with the receptionist, giving your name and phone number and the kind of work you're interested in. Ask about the next step in becoming a volunteer.

The agency may call back when you're not at a phone. But if you've asked some specific questions, the agency can leave information on your voice mail, if you have it, or with the person who answers the phone. Move the conversation along with each contact, even if you never get to talk to a "real" person.

The agency report form at the end of this chapter offers some good questions you can adapt for your conversations with an agency. If you are working with a program coordinator at your church or school, the information you gather in your phone conversation may help her or him develop and maintain a list of good agencies to work with. You can photocopy this form and give a copy to your coordinator, or keep it on hand for yourself if you get information on more than one agency.

Just remember—the fact that an organization does not call you back immediately does not mean the agency doesn't want you. If you haven't heard back in two or three days, call again. However, if you call back several times without getting a response, it may mean the agency is too disorganized to be a good option for you.

The Intake Process

Some groups will put you to work if you simply show up. However, many agencies have what they call an intake process. You may need to fill out an application form and perhaps have an interview. Some organizations that work with vulnerable people (children, people with disabilities, or the elderly) may ask you to fill out an extensive application and provide references. This will take extra time, but it's a sign that the agency is concerned about the people they serve. They're not being suspicious of you. They just want to do everything they can to make sure no one will get hurt.

The Interview

You can ask to meet with someone at the agency so you can get a feel for the place, or the volunteer coordinator may ask to meet with you. Set up an appointment, and then confirm you have the date, time, and place correct. Then remember to write down the information and put it somewhere where you can find it.

During your interview, the agency will be assessing whether you will be a good addition to their team. An interview or site visit is also a time for you to evaluate the organization. Service is a two-way street. Be conscious of your dress as you prepare for your interview. Depending on the setting, you may want to wear business or casual clothes. Dress in a manner that shows respect for the agency, the people it serves, and yourself.

Be prepared for questions the interviewer may ask, such as; "Why do you want to work here?" "What kind of work would you like to do?" "When are you available?" "What skills or experiences do you have that would be helpful?" Thinking about these questions before your interview will help you organize your thoughts. You might even want to write out your answers.

Be ready with your own questions, such as; "What are your expectations of volunteers?" "Will I have a supervisor?" "May I have a tour of the building?" "Do you have training, and if so, when is it available?" Good communication is very important to the success of a service project. Do everything you can to make clear what your expectations are, and to discover their expectations. If you realize after the interview is over that you've forgotten something, call the contact person and ask.

Evaluating the Agency

After your interview or site visit, take some time to evaluate the agency. You can use the following questions as a springboard.
- Did you feel safe?
- Did staff act respectfully toward clients?
- Was the staff person who met with you respectful toward you?
- Did you feel pressured to make a larger commitment than is possible?
- Will someone help you get started with your work?

What you are looking for is respect—respect for you and respect for the clients being served. A certain amount of disorganization is okay, as long as it doesn't make your job impossible.

Making a Commitment

Be realistic about what you can do. If you enjoy your work, at first you may want to go several times a week. An agency may be desperate for help and may encourage or even pressure you to come often. It is difficult to keep such a commitment. You may get burned out or end up neglecting school, family or friends. It is much better to start slowly than to get in over your head and have to bail out. Your school might limit the number of hours you can devote to volunteer work per week, so check ahead of time so the agency can accurately set expectations.

On the other hand, it may be difficult to stay with a commitment that is totally open ended. If you are working with a confirmation or school program that requires a specific number of hours, you may want to sign up with a program that has a clear schedule. For example, hospitals often require a regular commitment of four hours per week. That outside structure will help you get your hours in, especially if you have a busy schedule.

If You're on Your Own

If you are doing a project independent of any agency, you will want to be aware of some other things. Your project may be as simple as forming a relationship with one person and spending time with her or him or helping her or him learn a skill. Just be clear about how much time you can spend, and try to be clear with yourself about what you would like to accomplish. Your goals may well evolve as your relationship develops.

If you are taking on a more complicated project, keep these questions in mind:
- Whose help do I need to accomplish this project?
- Who would be good to speak with in order to develop ideas and a plan?
- Who might be interested in volunteering with me?
- What is your plan? How are you going to accomplish your goal?
- Are you sure people want the service you intend to provide? (Have you ever had a relative give you a gift you really didn't want? The same principle applies here.)
- Are there resources you will need to accomplish your plan? Where can you get them?
- Do you need permission from anyone—the city, your school, your parents—to take on this project?

Asking God for Help in Choosing

You may be feeling overwhelmed at the prospect of deciding on a project. There may be so many options available that you don't know how to choose. On the other hand, it may seem as though you can't find any workable options. Either way, a good first step is to ask God for help in making your selection. God loves the people you will serve and knows the challenges and joy that lies ahead. God knows the best path for you to walk.

One way of dealing with doubts about God is putting out a request and watching to see how God shows up. Take some time to ask for God's guidance in this decision. And then remember to pay attention, because that guidance may show up in pretty subtle ways. An unexpected opportunity may drop into your lap. Someone may make a chance comment that brings sudden clarity to your decision. You may be driving along a street and see a lonely child you hadn't noticed before. Some young people discover God's presence for the first time through service. Inviting God in on your selection process is the first opportunity for that to happen.

And Then There's Family

Service can be a great way to spend time with family. Doing service work with a parent or sibling gets you "points" in two directions: you're helping someone who needs you, and at the same time you are spending quality time with a parent or other members of your family. With today's busy lifestyles, family time can be hard to come by. Service can offer a great opportunity to get to know your family in new ways while enjoying their company.

Some projects, such as a crisis nursery or battered women's shelter, require that you serve with an adult. (Remember, an adult is someone over the age of eighteen.) Don't let that restriction stop you—there may well be an adult who would love to work with you.

Prayer

Now the boy Samuel was ministering to the Lord under Eli. . . . Samuel was lying down in the temple of the Lord, where the ark of God was. Then the Lord called, "Samuel! Samuel!" and he said, "Here I am!" and ran to Eli, and said, "Here I am, for you called me." But he said, "I did not call; lie down again." So he went and lay down. The Lord called again, "Samuel!" Samuel got up and went to Eli and said, "Here I am, for you called me." But he said, "I did not call, my son; lie down again." Now Samuel did not yet know the Lord, and the word of the Lord had not yet been revealed to him. The Lord called Samuel again, a third time. And he got up and went to Eli, and said, "Here I am, for you called me." Then Eli perceived that the Lord was calling the boy. Therefore Eli said to Samuel, "Go, lie down, and if he calls you, you shall say, 'Speak, Lord, for your servant is listening.'" So Samuel went and lay down in his place.

Now the Lord came and stood there, calling as before, "Samuel! Samuel!" And Samuel said, "Speak, for your servant is listening."

(1 Samuel 3:1–10)

Close with this or another prayer:

Lord,

Like Samuel, I don't always recognize your voice calling me. Please help me to learn to listen to your voice in my heart. Guide me as I discover the best path to take. Please bless my decisions and all the people I will meet in the months ahead. Help me, like Samuel, to be a sign of your presence to those around me. Amen.

Agency Report

Name of agency: _____

Agency address: _____

Contact person: _____

Phone number: _____

Date of call: _____

Types of services provided:

Are service opportunities available to teens?

What type of time commitment is expected of volunteers?

Is there an application process? How does it work?

Is training available or required? How does it work?

What else did you notice about the agency or its staff?

Chapter 3
GETTING READY

The Nuts and Bolts

Now that you've selected a project, you still have a few steps to complete before you begin. Being prepared and organized can help your transition into service. If you have your paperwork and permissions taken care of ahead of time, you can devote all your attention to the people you will meet. You can avoid wasting precious time going back and taking care of details, perhaps losing weeks that could be used for service.

Training and Orientation

Many organizations sponsor orientation programs where you can learn about the agency and your responsibilities. You will have the opportunity to meet staff and clients and to ask questions. If the agency does not offer an orientation, you can still ask to visit and tour the site. This added information will help you be more comfortable and become an effective volunteer more quickly. If the organization hosts a Web site, an online visit is another way to find valuable information as you begin your project.

Some organizations require not only an orientation but also a certain amount of formal training. For example, most hospitals require formal training for all their volunteers. The good news is that you will have a clear sense of your responsibilities before you begin; the bad news is training may be available only a few times a year. Be sure to call early if you plan to volunteer in a hospital or other organization that might require special training.

Written Agreements

It is a good idea to have a clear agreement with the agency about your time commitment and responsibilities. Some service projects go wrong because the agency or the student is not clear about the work to be done or the amount of time expected. Handout 1, "Agency Agreement," at the end of this chapter can help avoid any possible misunderstanding about expectations. You may also need an additional written agreement between you and your service coordinator. Handout 2, "Service Contract," at the end of the chapter is a good reminder of your responsibilities.

Documenting Your Hours

If you are serving required hours as part of a class or Confirmation program, be sure someone at the agency can verify your presence. Some students have been frustrated because they serve faithfully at an agency and then are unable to get credit for their hours because no one has kept a record of their time.

Many agencies have a formal sign-in and sign-out procedure for security reasons. If these records are retained, they can provide you with automatic verification of your hours. If there is no sign-in, ask a staff member to document your work—in other words, to provide a written verification of the hours you serve. Be sure to remember to check in and out with that person on your visits. If there is no outside adult who can witness to your work, a parent may be able to verify your hours.

It is always wise to keep your own record of your service work, just in case. Handout 3, "Service Hours Record," at the end of the chapter can be used for your own record-keeping. Why go to the trouble of documenting? A written record can give you the personal satisfaction of knowing just how much time you have given. You may be surprised as you watch the hours mount and be reminded of the impact you have been able to make.

On the other hand, keeping a written record can also be a reality check if you have been putting off your work or have been serving shorter shifts than originally planned. If you are required to serve a certain number of hours, keeping an up-to-date record can help you avoid panic at the end of the term.

Supporting College and Job Applications

Colleges and employers pay attention to volunteer work. Service is a sign of responsibility, generosity, and character. Many students find service gives them an opportunity to demonstrate talents and abilities not necessarily reflected in grade point averages or in test scores.

Young people have discovered and developed abilities in coaching, art, computers, construction, and other areas through service. Documenting your service hours is one way to let a college or an employer know of talents and skills you possess outside of the classroom.

Some schools put service hours on all transcripts. If yours does not, you can still ask to have your work kept in your file so colleges and employers have access to the information.

The President's Volunteer Service Award is given to high school students who serve one hundred or more hours in a year. An organization such as a church or school applies to become a certifying organization, they then verify your service hours and apply for the award for you. The award itself is a great affirmation of your generosity, and at the same time it is a valuable addition to a college or job application.

Your Parents

Do you need permission from anyone to complete your project? If you need to be released from school to do your service, make sure you go through the proper channels to approve your absence. A school, parish, or service agency may require a parental release form. Handout 4, "Parent Permission Form," at the end of this chapter verifies that your parents are informed of your plans and have given their consent. The form also provides important emergency information in case something unexpected happens.

Be sure your parents know where you are serving and what you will be doing. As mentioned in chapter 2, you may want to consider inviting your parents to join you. Your service project has the potential to change your life; by inviting others to come on board you increase your ability to have an impact. Many parents have become committed to a cause as a result of their children's service work. Service often acts like a pebble tossed into water; ripples expand and touch others in ways you did not anticipate when you were just starting out.

Staying Safe

Some students serve in neighborhoods that experience street violence. If you do not live in a similar neighborhood, you may need to learn to take precautions that are unfamiliar to you. In the beginning, you may not know or understand the unspoken rules that govern a new setting. Chapter 7 can help you be conscious of unwritten rules about behavior and help you learn those rules more quickly. Knowing how to handle yourself can help you avoid unpleasantness and stay out of danger.

In the interests of both promptness and safety, plan your route ahead of time so you don't get lost. Lock your doors when you get into your car. In some areas, locked doors are an important safety precaution, but the click of doors locking as your car slows to a stop next to a stranger can appear disrespectful. Be alert to your surroundings and walk with purpose. Avoid being alone on the street at night. If someone confronts you, avoid escalating the situation. Many people know to practice these precautions automatically. If these habits are new to you, you will find they come in handy in other situations as well.

These paragraphs are not intended to reinforce negative stereotypes about our central cities. Many people who live in rural areas or the suburbs are afraid of neighborhoods that are in fact safe. One of the values of service is expanding the part of the world we consider "ours." Your service coordinator, youth minister, or adult mentor can be a valuable resource in balancing generosity with prudence. Your parents may have concerns about the location of your service work. If your parents are concerned, invite them to visit the site with you and to talk with your service coordinator or an agency representative.

Transportation and Scheduling

You may need to be creative about transportation. If you don't have a car but want to work at a distance from your home, try to persuade someone with a car to serve with you. Ask your leader for names of other students serving in the same agency, and see if you can ride along. Try riding the bus if you live in the city and haven't done so in the past. Think outside the box, and don't give up on a project you want just because you have trouble finding transportation.

Preparing Yourself for the Experience

Your attitude will have a big impact on your success. You can prepare yourself for the best possible service experience by taking some time now to open your eyes and your heart to the people you will meet.

The People You Will Serve

Most readers of this book will serve people or be in a setting that is unfamiliar to them. For example, many teenagers have very little contact with small children. Others might not have had much contact with the elderly. Perhaps you will be working with people with disabilities that are new to you. Take a few moments to jot down your thoughts about the people you will work with and the setting where you will find yourself. We will refer back to these pages as you gain new experience and have the chance to adjust your ideas.

Who will you be working with in your project? (for example, children, the elderly, nursing home residents, and so on)

Briefly describe what you expect to encounter in your work. What do you expect will be appealing about the people with whom you will be working? What do you expect will be challenging? What are you looking forward to? What are you feeling apprehensive about?

Now do a bit of research. Search the Internet, keying in phrases such as "Caring for elderly" or "Down's syndrome" or "children and reading." Look for information about those you will soon be meeting and ways you can help. You can also interview others who have knowledge and experience in your new field. You can ask other students with volunteer experience, your service coordinator, or another adult. Ask them to describe their experience.

Giving and Receiving

Many people say after a volunteer experience, "I thought I was there to give, but I discovered I received much more than I gave back." The primary goal of service is to meet needs in our community. We are there to share our resources—our time, our talents and skills, our concern—with others. They will also share their resources with us.

Service is a partnership. We are not doing things for other people; we are working with people. It is extremely important not to fall into an attitude of feeling better than those we serve. You will almost certainly find unexpected gifts among the people you serve. Indeed, discovering those gifts often draws people to continue to volunteer long after their school or church project is over. The gifts you may experience include:

- a sense of humor
- a new view of yourself
- a new appreciation of the important things in life
- courage and optimism in the face of challenges
- unconditional love
- an open and unself-conscious faith in God
- a new and positive humility

The list is open ended. As you begin, look for opportunities to remember that you are a partner with the people you will meet. Be conscious of listening, of being open, of being ready to receive as well as give.

What gifts do you think the people you meet will be able to offer you?

Prayer

"It is not enough for us to say, "I love God,"
but I also have to love my neighbor.
St. John says that you are a liar
if you say you love God and you don't love your neighbor.
How can you love God, whom you do not see,
if you do not love your neighbor whom you see,
whom you touch, with whom you live?
And so it is very important for us to realize

that love, to be true, has to hurt.
I must be willing to give whatever it takes
not to harm other people
and, in fact, to do good to them.
This requires that I be willing to give until it hurts.
Otherwise, there is not true love in me
and I bring injustice, not peace, to those around me.

(Mother Teresa, "National Prayer Breakfast," February 4, 1994)

Close with this or another prayer:
Dear God,
Please help me to be willing to love the people I am about to meet. Help me to learn to give what they need, even if it means sacrifice or discomfort. Show me your way to love, and please help me learn from those around me.
Amen.

Agency Agreement

I, (student name) _____, commit to work

(number of hours, total or per week) _____ at (name of agency

or project) _____.

I commit to the following:
1. I will serve at the times agreed upon between myself and the service agency.
2. I will notify the agency of any absences at least one day in advance. I will make
    arrangements with my supervisor to make up the missed time if appropriate.
3. I will attend all scheduled meetings and training sessions related to my service
    commitment. In the event of unavoidable conflicts, I will notify the agency to set
    up an alternative time to meet.
4. I will be responsible for having all required forms, recommendations, and evalua-
    tions completed and handed in to the agency.

_____

Student signature

_____

Supervisor signature

Service Contract

I, (student name) _____, commit to work

(number of hours, total or per week) _____. at (name of

agency or project) _____.

I understand that I am to fulfill the following requirements:

1. I will meet all deadlines in an appropriate manner. Any change must be arranged with the program leader.
2. I am responsible for notifying the service agency of any absences. I will make arrangements with my supervisor to make up the missed time if appropriate.
3. I will attend all scheduled meetings related to the service program. In the event of unavoidable conflicts, I will notify the program leader to set up an alternative time to meet with the program leader.
4. I will be responsible for having all required forms, reports, and evaluations completed and handed in to the program leader.

_____
Signature

Service Hours Record

Name: _____

Agency or Project: _____

Date	Hours Served	Description of Activity

Parent Permission Form

I, (parent/guardian) _____ grant permission for (student's name) _____ to participate in service at (name of agency or location) _____. In consideration of my child's participation, I agree to indemnify _____ from any claim or lawsuit brought against _____ by myself, my child, or others, that arise out of any behavior by my child at the above activity.

Emergency Medical Treatment: In the event of an emergency, I give permission to transport my child to a hospital for emergency medical treatment. I wish to be advised prior to any further treatment by a doctor or a hospital. In the event of an emergency, please contact:

Parent/Guardian: _____ (w) _____

(h) _____

(c) _____

If unable to reach, contact: _____   _____

                (Name)   (Phone)

Optional medical information: _____   _____

                 (Family Doctor)   (Phone)

Medication or other health concerns: _____

As parent/guardian, I agree to all of the above-stated considerations and conditions.

_____   _____

(Parent/Guardian Signature)   (Date)

Chapter 4
STARTING OUT

Getting Started

It's time to begin. You've selected your project, made a commitment, gotten permission, found transportation. Now you get to show up. You get to meet the people you will be working with. You get to start the process of discovering what you have to offer in this new environment.

Being Comfortable with Who You Are

Perhaps your project is a continuation of work you already know. You're working in the parish nursery, and you've already done a lot of baby-sitting. You're volunteering in a nursing home, and you already have a great relationship with a grandparent who is ill. In these cases, you're probably feeling fairly confident as you begin. Many readers will be trying something new, serving people with whom they are unfamiliar or providing a service that is new to them. It's easy to feel unsure of oneself and to compare oneself with more experienced folks.

> "Never doubt that a small group of thoughtful, committed people can change the world. Indeed, it is the only thing that ever has." (Margaret Mead)

You may watch staff members or other volunteers who are clearly comfortable and successful in this new setting. They are friendly and outgoing—joking and laughing with people they don't know, setting you and other newcomers immediately at ease. They may be quiet and empathetic, able to get shy children to trust them and relax, responding kindly even under stressful circumstances. They may understand the agency and the circumstances of their clients in ways that seem beyond you. You are left wondering how you can ever measure up and what you could possibly contribute.

They have their own gifts. You have yours. You bring something unique and irreplaceable to this venture. There are people who need exactly what you have to offer. You can learn from other people without having to be them. Years ago, I volunteered in a center for children with mental and physical disabilities. One little boy, Alan, had severe cerebral palsy. I was assigned to feed him, spend time with him, and get him and the other children ready for their session in the pool. Alan was not well cared for at home and seemed very fragile. His arms were held tightly against his chest and his legs were rigid. At pool time I slowly and carefully took off his clothes and put on his swimsuit, and was rewarded by his beautiful smile.

The first time I brought Alan to the pool, I was stunned. A young college student took Alan in his arms and then began bobbing and swishing him around vigorously in the water. Grinning, he would prop Alan's arms up on the side of the pool and challenge him to pull himself out of the water. Alan would try hopelessly, giggling hysterically all the while.

This volunteer was able to bring out Alan's capacity for play and struggle. I was able to give Alan quiet attention and comfort. He needed both. He needed both of us. I could appreciate the gifts of the other volunteer and learn that Alan was not as fragile as I'd thought—without having to become someone who teased and roughhoused.

Remember, you will grow and develop in your ability as a volunteer. You will find new capacities you didn't know you had. It's impossible to know at this point what your experience will call from you. Just keep this in mind: Learn from the people around you. Don't measure yourself against them. One supervisor gave this rough paraphrase of Jesus's message to all new volunteers. Her words: "Just show up—and then love them." Your presence and your care are the greatest gifts you can bring.

Finding a Mentor

You may have a designated supervisor—someone whose job it is to answer your questions, show you around, and keep track of the time you serve. Whether or not someone is officially assigned to that role, it can be very helpful to find someone willing to act as a mentor for you.

A mentor is someone with wisdom and experience who will take an interest in you and your new role. A mentor can help you develop your own style of working with people and can identify challenges before they present themselves and advise you on how to handle them. A mentor can simply be there for you. On a difficult day, a mentor can pick you up, encourage you, and remind you that tomorrow will be better. A mentor rejoices in your victories—times when you've stretched yourself, or when you've really touched another person. And a mentor will help hold you accountable on days when you're tempted to give less than your best.

Anyone can be a mentor—another volunteer, a secretary, someone working in maintenance. The person assigned to be your supervisor may not have enough time to work well as a mentor for you. Asking for help from someone will enable you to help others more effectively—so speak up.

Dealing with Absences

Absences when you're volunteering are in a class by themselves. If you don't show up for a scheduled shift at a job at McDonald's, you create a problem. Other people need to cover for you and do your work. Money could be lost and customers disappointed. Showing up is important. But when you are working with a group of vulnerable children or adults, failure to show up can be a crushing disappointment to them. Your visit may be the highlight of their week. If you are dealing with children, you may be one of the few trustworthy people in their lives who pay attention to them. If you promise to be there and then don't show up, a vulnerable person can experience a significant blow to his or her ability to trust—in people and in the world.

Schedules change and things come up. You may not be able to serve when you'd planned, but be sure to call and let someone know you will not be there. Some programs take this so seriously that absence without notification results in expulsion from the program or failure of a class. The consequence is very serious, but it's an indication of just how important you can be in someone else's life.

Expectations and Reality

Before your first day volunteering you have probably imagined what people will be like and how you'll behave. What you encounter will probably be different. It may be more fun than you expected; it may be tougher than you'd hoped. You may be given more responsibility than you'd realized. Allow time for your expectations to adjust to reality. Just because an assignment is not what you expected doesn't mean it won't be great. It may just take time.

Dilemmas That Might Arise

We have been speaking of taking care of the last few details that can help you get off to the very best start possible. But for most people, challenges will arise. Part of the growth that happens through service is learning to deal with difficulties. The following pages give you tips on some of the most common challenges encountered by new volunteers.

Handling Conflict

You may run into or observe conflict with staff, other volunteers, or clients. Culture shapes the ways people handle conflict. In some cultures, people tend to be loud, direct, and confrontational. Other cultures encourage people to handle conflict indirectly. You may discover you are offending people by being direct, or you may be feeling intimidated by people who move in close to you, make direct eye contact, and raise their voices when you do something they don't like.

Assertive communication is a style of dealing with conflict that can be helpful anywhere, although you may vary your approach depending on your setting and your own personality and experience.

A brief summary of assertive communication includes five steps. A conversation would not necessarily cover the steps in this order, and you might not say each step out loud. But using this procedure can help you be clear about your message and hold your own in the face of resistance.

1. Describe what is happening that concerns you. Be careful to describe only what you can actually observe. For example, you can't really observe whether someone is listening to you or not. Listening is an attitude, and we can't directly see or hear an attitude. You can observe that a person doesn't make eye contact, interrupts you when you try to speak, talks about something else when you finish speaking. Assertive communication describes what is clearly observable—specific words or behavior. This step takes practice but can be very helpful in not escalating a situation.

2. Name how you feel about what's going on. Depending on the situation, you may or may not want to actually tell the other person what you are feeling. However, being aware of your own feelings will help you manage them more effectively. If you're feeling angry, you can easily escalate a situation unnecessarily. Usually when people feel angry they're responding to another emotion that occurred first. For example, if a child you're tutoring won't work on the lesson and tears up his paper, you may feel angry. But beneath the anger is probably some fear that you won't be able to handle the situation, some confusion about what to do, some disappointment and hurt that your efforts to help are being rejected. Naming those feelings, at least to yourself, can help you detach from them and communicate more effectively.

3. Explain why you're concerned. For example, you could say, "I'm concerned that if I can't find someone to document my hours each week I won't get credit for them for my class." This is much better than saying, "Nobody is ever here when I need them. You don't seem to care that I might flunk my class because you're not here when you're supposed to be." Be careful not to escalate a situation by using loaded words like never and always, or labeling people with words like selfish or irresponsible.

4. Ask for a specific change in behavior. For example, with an uncooperative child, asking that they "behave" may not help them understand what you want. Suggesting the child work on the lesson for 10 minutes, and then laying your watch on the table so he or she can see his or her progress, can offer a concrete suggestion he or she feels he or she can follow.

5. Provide consequences if necessary. Most of us are familiar with consequences as a form of discipline. We're generally not accustomed to giving consequences to people our own age and even less to people in authority. But if, for example, an agency keeps scheduling you for more hours than you can serve, you may need to inform them that you will need to either not come for some assigned shifts or find another opportunity. If consequences are discussed without anger, they can be an effective way of dealing with conflict. And they can provide you with a solution even if the other person doesn't respond to your attempt to communicate.

Practice Dealing with Conflict

Choose an example of a conflict occurring in your service work or in your life at the moment. It could involve someone you're serving, a supervisor, or another volunteer. It could be a situation in your family, with friends, or in a job, a sport, or a school activity.

1. What exactly is bothering you? What is the other person doing that you would like to see changed? Remember to describe only things you can observe directly with your senses. Describe behavior rather than your interpretation of behavior.
2. How are you feeling about the situation? What emotions are you experiencing in addition to anger or frustration? disappointment? confusion? embarrassment?
3. Why do you think the problem exists? What might you be contributing to the situation? Remember not to use language that will put the other person on the defensive.
4. What specifically would you like changed? Be realistic, but don't sell yourself short, either.
5. Are there consequences that would be appropriate in this situation? Are you willing to impose those consequences?

Assertive communication, rather than being aggressive or passive, provides a means of standing up for yourself or someone else while still being respectful.

Holding People Accountable

You may be asked to hold some people accountable in the course of your work. For example, if you are dealing with children, you probably need to get them to engage in an activity, treat one another and you respectfully, and clean up after themselves.

When people are uncooperative, you need to hold them accountable. This is a matter of having respect for yourself, others, and for whatever activity you have been assigned. Holding people accountable can be done using the same communication techniques we just mentioned. When people misbehave, whether adults or children, there is usually a reason. Some do it for attention, others for power, others because they are unhappy in their lives and are acting out their sadness and anger in this setting, and still others because they have given up on themselves. Sometimes it's more simple—they simply don't like what they're being asked to do.

If someone repeatedly acts out in a certain way, a key to changing their behavior can be to figure out the goal of their misbehavior and then try to redirect that goal. For example, if a child has learned to get attention by misbehaving, work to pay attention to good behavior. If an elderly resident has a strong need to control, figure out how to avoid a power struggle and still maintain the control you need over your time together. Figuring this out is a challenge, and you won't always be successful, but the skill is one you'll carry into other parts of your life.

Setting Boundaries

It is important that you feel safe both emotionally and physically in your new environment. You may work with people who mean you no harm but who make you feel uncomfortable and you're not sure why. Boundaries are invisible barriers that keep us safe from other people and from difficult situations. Some groups of people either have different boundaries or have personal difficulty respecting boundaries. People with mental disabilities, for example, often have trouble recognizing the need for boundaries. They may ask personal questions, or hug or touch inappropriately.

Children have imperfectly formed boundaries, especially if their families have not taught them effectively. They may pull or climb on you incessantly or demand physical affection that you do not have the time or inclination to give. Boundaries also vary among cultures and different areas of the country.

Physical boundaries are respected when people do not physically hurt, intimidate, or annoy others. Our physical boundaries also include maintaining a comfortable distance between ourselves and other people. You have a right to ask people to keep a proper distance from you. Volunteering does not require that you allow people to touch you or hug you if you prefer they would not.

Emotional boundaries concern things like sharing personal information, expressions of affection, or becoming involved in people's lives outside of the agency. The needs you see around you can be so overwhelming that you begin to feel a responsibility to take care of everyone's problems. You have a right—and a responsibility—to protect your own boundaries and to ask for help if someone does not respect your attempts to hold that line. It is important to keep a realistic picture of your own strengths and resources, and to keep appropriate boundaries as a volunteer.

You may be tempted to cross boundaries out of compassion for the people you serve. You may want to develop a personal relationship with someone you meet through your work, or to help them outside of your time at the agency. It would be wise to get advice from your parents or a mentor. Because of your unfamiliarity with this new setting, this may be more complicated than it seems.

What are some examples of issues with boundaries that you have observed? What would you recommend to the people involved?

What If It Doesn't Work Out?

Not everyone falls in love on the first date. Not every service project feels like a match on the first visit. Or the second. Or even, perhaps, the third or fourth. Lots of people feel uncomfortable the first two or three times on a service project and still go on to love their work.

If you start to be concerned that you are in the wrong place, talk to your supervisor or your service coordinator. She or he may be able to offer some tips to help you adjust to your new project. Or perhaps another assignment in the same agency will suit you better. Give yourself four or five sessions before deciding you want to switch projects. But then, if it still seems like a bad fit, consider finding a new opportunity. Be sure to leave respectfully. Let people know you will not be coming back. You don't have an obligation to explain why, but you will be helping them by doing so. For example, if you leave an agency because they are not providing you with the support you need to do a good job, it would be valuable for them to know that. It can be an opportunity to try assertive communication.

Don't let an unfortunate match turn you sour on serving. There is an opportunity out there that is a match for you. There is a service project you can love and that will use your time and talents well. A great match is worth searching out.

Finding Guidance and Strength Through Prayer

You will most likely be challenged and encounter the unexpected in the work you are about to do. When we meet difficulties, it helps to look to agency staff, a service coordinator, or a friend for advice. It is also important to remember that God offers us strength and guidance when we face difficult times.

Even people who pray often can forget to really open themselves up to God's help. Sometimes prayer is like a checklist, where we instruct God on what we think he should do in a certain situation. For example:

> God, please help Lisa be more cooperative. Please help her sit still and listen to me and concentrate on her homework. Please stop her from getting angry when I tell her she needs to finish the lesson before she can have her snack.

There's nothing wrong with that prayer. However it doesn't fully open the door to God's help. We've got the solution, and we're just looking for God to make it happen. It's kind of like asking a friend for advice but not being interested in the answer.

Another form of prayer opens our minds and gives God more room to help us. We can follow several steps that may help us see more responses to our prayer. Gratitude is a good way to start.

- Begin by remembering the blessings in our work. This will shift our focus to a more positive way of looking at a situation, even a tough one.
- The next step is to name what's going on with us—our feelings and concerns. At this point we are getting clearer in our own minds just exactly why we need God's help.
- Third, we open ourselves up to God's guidance. We try to let go, for the moment, of our own assessment of the situation. Just as when you ask a friend's advice you open yourself to their perspective, we try to open ourselves to God's perspective.
- Fourth, we make a request. We ask for what we need. Most of us have had lots of practice with this.
- Fifth, we "sign off."
- And finally, we stay open after we finish praying, staying alert to any new information that may present itself.

Such a prayer might look like this:

> God,
>
> [Gratitude] Thank you for this day and the chance to be of service. Thank you for the opportunity to be with Lisa and get to know her.
>
> [Naming the situation and our feelings] You know that we've had a couple of challenging lessons and that I'm feeling frustrated and confused.
>
> [Opening ourselves to God's guidance] Please help me to see Lisa as you do. Please open my mind to know her better and to find new ways to work with her. Help me to recognize anything I may be doing that's contributing to the problem.
>
> [Request] Please help Lisa be able to focus on her lesson. Help her to know that I'm here to help her, and to learn to handle her frustration in different ways.
>
> [Sign off] Thank you for the love you have for me and for Lisa.
> Amen.

Sometimes we think prayers go unanswered because we pray and then forget to pay attention to what happens. If we simply ask God to change a situation and don't notice a difference, we think God has not listened to or answered us. Sometimes God sends an answer and we're not paying close enough attention and miss it.

For example, God might answer this prayer by prompting our math teacher to talk about a teaching strategy in class that we could apply to our situation. If we forget to pay attention after we're done praying, we may not make the connection between the teacher's comment and the work we're doing.

Prayer

The spirit of the Lord God is upon me,
>because the Lord has anointed me;
>
>he has sent me to bring good news to the oppressed,
>>to bind up the brokenhearted,
>>to proclaim liberty to the captives,
>>>and release to the prisoners.

(Isaiah 61:1)

Close with this or another prayer:

Jesus,

You were sent to bring light into the world, to comfort those who are sad and bring hope to those who are discouraged. Please help me follow your example as I begin this work. Please help me to find the gifts you have given me and to share them with those I meet. Please help me see your face in the people I serve.

Amen.

Chapter 5
CATHOLIC SOCIAL TEACHING

The Catholic Church's Vision

Many people with generous hearts give themselves in service every day. They serve for a variety of reasons. Some give simply out of human concern, because they want to share their gifts and relieve the suffering they see around them.

Some people's motivation and vision has another dimension. People of faith, whether Buddhist, Muslim, Christian, or any other religion can help others as an expression of their faith. Each faith tradition has its own way of talking about and viewing the responsibility to put beliefs into action.

The Catholic Church's vision is called Catholic social teaching. This teaching is based in Scripture and is expressed in Church documents such as formal statements by popes and bishops and council declarations. From its beginning, Scripture has been very clear about our responsibility to those who are vulnerable and economically poor.

The Church also has a long tradition of outreach. Members of the early Church pooled their money and property, using their resources to care for the poor. In the Middle Ages, convents and monasteries were places of hospitality, healing, and sanctuary. Often the church was people's only recourse when they needed help. Saints throughout the ages have set heroic examples, from Saint Elizabeth of Hungary to Saint John Baptist de La Salle to venerable Mother Teresa.

Christianity Untried

Chesterton says:
"The Christian ideal has not been tried and found wanting.
It has been found difficult and left untried."

Christianity has not been tried because people thought it was impractical.

And men have tried everything except Christianity.
And everything that men have tried has failed.

(Peter Maurin, *Easy Essays*)

1. What are some of Jesus's sayings that people have considered impractical? "Turn the other cheek" and "love your enemies" are a few examples. Do you consider them impractical?

2. *Found wanting* means to be considered inadequate. What would a truly Christian society look like?

Individual or Social Morality?

What comes to mind when you hear the word *morality?* Often we think first of lying, stealing, or sexual decisions. These are examples of individual morality, which governs people's relationships with other individuals or small groups of people. Social morality sets guidelines for relationships among larger groups of people. For example, in the Old Testament, God frequently admonished the Jews on their treatment of widows, orphans, aliens, and the poor in their midst. As our world has grown more interdependent, and the population and nations have grown, the Church has needed to apply the principles revealed in Scripture to the complex issues of today.

When the Scriptures were written, we did not know about embryonic stem cell research, global warming, nuclear weapons, and countless other things. In its social teaching the Church has distilled the core message of Scripture and applied it to today. In 1997, the United States Conference of Catholic Bishops (USCCB) sent out a message, *Sharing Catholic Social Teaching*, to all Catholic schools and parishes. The bishops stated all Catholic education needs to include this essential tradition of Catholic social thought. The bishops reviewed the extensive resources on the topic and summarized it in seven central principles:

1. human life and dignity
2. the call to family, community, and participation
3. rights and responsibilities
4. the option for the poor and vulnerable
5. the dignity of work and the rights of workers
6. solidarity
7. care for God's creation

Although it is not included in the bishops' statement, an eighth principle— the need to be peacemakers in the world—is often accepted based on a careful reading of the Scriptures and the teaching of the Church.

Why Talk About Catholic Social Teaching?

The principles act as a lens, or a way of looking at the world. The way we look at things often shapes how we behave. For example, a good coach inspires participants to find their unique gifts, work hard, and compete honestly because they see the talents of the athlete, the joy of the game, and the chance to make a difference in someone's life. Coaches often have catchphrases that participants can easily remember on the field or in the middle of an intense debate. The Special Olympics developed a pledge for developmentally disabled athletes competing in the Special Olympics, "Let me win, but if I cannot win, let me be brave in the attempt." That phrase has carried many athletes farther than they ever thought possible.

The principles are like these catchphrases. If they become part of us, they shape the way we react to situations, particularly situations that are unjust. Why should you accept these particular catchphrases? You can examine the principles simply as a philosophy you may or may not agree with. You can also examine them as part of the package that goes with being Catholic.

Catholic social teaching has been called "the church's best-kept secret." Nobody is deliberately keeping these ideas secret. The good word just hasn't been told as often as it should. Most people know the Church's stand on premarital sex or embryonic stem cell research, however many people don't know about the powerful message the Church teaches on our behavior toward one another and Creation. Being Catholic does not just shape our behavior on Sunday mornings. Being Catholic calls us to go beyond ourselves; it influences our relationship with God and with one another in all aspects of our lives.

How Do We Apply the Principles?

These eight principles sound rather vague. There are many books and classes designed just to help people understand them. We cannot do them justice in this one short chapter, but we can make a start. The principles of Catholic social teaching become clearer when we contrast them with some attitudes commonly held in our society. The table below lists each principle with a brief explanation, contrasted against a common attitude.

<u>Catholic Social Teaching Principles</u>	<u>Common North American Cultural Attitudes</u>
1. Human life and dignity All human beings are sacred, from the time of conception until natural death, because they are created by God.	Human beings have value because they are productive, and their lives can be terminated or devalued because of illness, disability, poverty, quality of life, or behavior.
2. The call to family, community, and participation Human beings are social. They are called to live in community and to use their gifts for their own enrichment and for the common good.	Protecting individual freedom is the highest value.
3. Rights and responsibilities Human beings have rights in accordance with their dignity as children of God. Each right carries a corresponding responsibility.	People have an absolute right to pursue their own goals as they see fit, as long as there is no serious, obvious harm to others.

Catholic Social Teaching Principles	**Common North American Cultural Attitudes**
4. The option for the poor and vulnerable As long as serious inequities exist in allocation of power and resources, Christians are called to give particular care to those who have less.	A democratic society and free economy ensure equal opportunity to acquire resources for all. People's only responsibility is to be reasonably truthful in negotiation.
5. The dignity of work and the rights of workers Work is not simply a commodity to be exchanged for a wage. Workers share in God's creative action and have a right to a living wage.	Work is a commodity to be bought and sold at current market value. An employer's only obligation is to pay the employee the promised wage.
6. Solidarity God's love is not limited by barriers of race, nation, or geographical distance. People are all responsible for one another.	At most, people are required to take care of those close to them—those who are similar because of race, geographical, or cultural proximity.
7. Care for God's creation The universe is created by God and loaned to people for their prudent use. They are to be good stewards of Creation, mindful of generations to follow.	The earth and space belong to the present generation to use as they see fit. Future generations more or less can take care of themselves.
8. Peacemaking Christians are called to be peacemakers out of respect for the dignity of each person as a child of God. The possible justifications for aggression are limited to such situations as immediate self-defense and the protection of the innocent.	Peace is better than war, but war is a legitimate means to protect immediate or distant economic or security interests. (Adapted from Constance Fourré, *Journey to Justice*, page 6)

The next pages take each principle individually and ask you to apply it to current questions. The issues are complex, and most often answers are not obvious. Two well-intended people who accept Catholic social teaching can still come up with different solutions to a dilemma. Try wrestling with these questions on your own, and then if possible see how your answers compare with those of others.

Human Life and Dignity

All of Catholic social teaching rests on this foundational principle: Every human being is a child of God. Every human being is sacred regardless of age, stage of development, gifts or disabilities, or what they have done. Jesus died for every person ever created. All people are precious in God's eyes, and we have a responsibility to recognize their value and treat them accordingly.

- What would this principle have to say about the death penalty? Would the severity of a person's crime make a difference? What is your opinion on the death penalty?

- What would this principle have to say about embryonic stem cell research? This research uses cells harvested from embryos created in a laboratory. What would the contrasting cultural attitude recommend? Why? What do you think?

The Call to Family, Community, and Participation

Americans take pride in our rugged individualism and self-reliance: in making it on our own, being able to make our own choices. People coming here from other countries are often astonished at the degree to which we prize individuality, often at the cost of community. This principle reminds us that we can become truly ourselves only in relationship with others. We have a responsibility to structure our society in such a way that all people are cared for and allowed to participate in community. Making decisions with "the common good" at heart means we are willing to sacrifice our own immediate interests for the benefit of others. If this principle is followed, we know we can count on the community to care for us if we are in need.

- What does this principle have to say about being an active citizen, exercising the right to vote, and working to bring about change in our society? What does the corresponding cultural attitude say? Why? What do you think?

- Some children in the United States go to schools where there is violence, where textbooks are outdated, where roofs leak, and where teachers may not even show up for class. What does this principle say about society's responsibility to these children? What does the corresponding cultural attitude say? Why? What do you think?

Rights and Responsibilities

How many times have you heard someone, or you yourself, start a statement with, "I have a right to . . ." Rights are important, and when our rights are violated we usually feel outraged. That sense of outrage provides the basis for a passion for justice, but we can forget that rights carry responsibilities. If I have a right to free speech, I also have a responsibility to protect your right to speak as well.

I have a responsibility to speak respectfully even if I disagree passionately. If I have a right to own property, I have a responsibility to protect your property as well. When Americans speak of rights, we think most readily of political rights: the right to free speech, the freedom of religion, the right to have a lawyer represent you if you are accused of a crime. All human beings have rights as children of God. These include economic rights: the right to adequate food, clothing, shelter, and health care. And with these rights come corresponding responsibilities.

- What does this principle say about the rights and responsibilities in a family? According to the principle, what would be the rights of parents? of children in relationship to parents? of children in relationship to one another? What do you think?

- How does the question of rights and responsibilities show up in the area where you serve? What are your rights and responsibilities in that situation? Are there any ways these rights and responsibilities are not being observed? Is there anything you can do about it?

The Option for the Poor and Vulnerable

This principle holds that we have a special responsibility to care for those who have fewer resources and less power. Some people find this principle confusing because it seems to favor one group over another. Consider a family who has a child with Down's syndrome. In order to develop to her or his maximum, that child needs to receive special therapy and education from an early age. A child needs to be shown repeatedly how to dress, how to handle himself or herself in public. The child may need to learn sign language before he or she learns to speak, which requires other members of the family to learn sign language as well. Is this fair? Of course. Families who have children with special needs must watch that other family members' needs don't get ignored, but more of the family's time, attention, and financial resources will be spent on caring for the particular needs of that child than on others. Similarly, in the human family some people have greater needs because they are economically poor or have other challenges. As a society, a human family, we have a responsibility to look out in a particular way for the vulnerable in our midst.

- What does this principle say about a family that cannot afford to care well for a child with disabilities? What is the responsibility of society in this situation? How does this principle build on the first principle—the dignity of each person?

- What might this principle say is the responsibility of society to children who are being abused in their families? Caring for children outside of their homes and providing them with resources to recover from abuse is expensive. Government support of these programs does require the use of tax money and might mean the raising of taxes or require tax money to be taken from other programs. How would you reasonably apply this principle?

The Dignity of Work and the Rights of Workers

We often think of work as just something we do to get money. Catholic social teaching tells us that work is one of the ways we express ourselves; it is a way we share in God's work of creation. Think of an activity you love: music, sports, education, or art. In an ideal world, everyone would be able to earn a living by doing work he or she loved. Some of you will be fortunate enough to find a career in work you love and know is worthwhile. Many jobs are not pleasant or interesting. They also have dignity because they contribute to the common good. Workers have dignity, both because they are God's children and because they are contributing needed services to society. Catholic social teaching tells us that all work has dignity and that workers should be treated with respect, paid a fair wage, and provided with humane working conditions.

- What would this principle say about the current minimum wage? Is it possible for a person to have a reasonable standard of living working forty hours per week at minimum wage? Is it possible for two working parents to support a family on two minimum-wage salaries?

Solidarity

The principle of solidarity reminds us we are all brothers and sisters. It is easy for us to be more concerned about events happening in our own community or our own country than in far-off places. For example, many countries have lived with terrorism for years. For most Americans, the attack on the World Trade Center was the first time that the horror of terrorism really hit home emotionally. Solidarity reminds us that race, geography, and ethnic background make no difference in our responsibility to care for one another. We share as much concern for Muslims, Buddhists, and nonbelievers as we do for other Christians. People who speak, dress, and behave differently from ourselves deserve as many resources and as much dignity and respect as we do.

*   What would this principle say about the question of people crossing the border from Mexico into the United States to seek work and send money back to support their families, whether or not they have proper documentation?

*   Consider this scenario: Over the last seventy-five years, a town has grown up around a large factory. A large percentage of the town's occupants work in the factory, finding jobs right after high school. The company decides to close the factory and have the work done in another country, where wages are less than half of those paid in the United States. How does this principle apply to a person who has worked in this factory for forty years, if there are no other jobs available in the town?

Care for God's Creation

It is easy for us to feel we own the earth, or at least the land we live on and the possessions we have purchased. Catholic social teaching reminds us that we are simply stewards, given only temporary use of the earth. We have a responsibility to Creation because it is valuable in itself, and we have a responsibility to coming generations who will need a healthy, sustainable planet on which to live. We care for Creation or damage it in choices we make about consumption, packaging, and recycling. We make choices in the amount of gasoline we use. As a society we make choices in the policies we set for companies that pollute our air or water and what land we preserve or develop. It is easy to think of environmentalism as simply "doing without." Being aware of the environment can also help us appreciate and enjoy what we have. It's like eating a bunch of junk food while you're watching TV, talking on the phone, and doing homework versus sitting down and really tasting an apple. You can consume a lot of calories without really enjoying any of them and do your body a disservice at the same time. Or you can save money and enjoy life by being more careful about your choices.

- Who is a person you know who is a conscious consumer, making careful decisions about not wasting resources?

- What is this person's attitude toward the earth? Do they seem to enjoy the things they consume more? less? the same as other people? Is there anything you can learn from this person?

Peacemaking

This principle follows naturally from the first, the sacred dignity of each human life. There is a lot of debate within the Church about just what this principle means. Some people say Catholic social teaching calls us to refuse to wage war under any circumstances. Others appeal to a tradition in the Church that gives standards for assessing whether a war is just. Both sides agree we should actively promote peaceful methods of resolving differences to the utmost.

A bumper sticker says, "If you want peace, work for justice." Wars are usually fought over land or resources. Obeying this principle would require countries to be just in their dealings with one another. Just relations among countries would eliminate many of the situations that lead to war. We can also be people of peace in our everyday relationships. We develop our attitudes about big issues through our habits on small issues.

- What are opportunities for peacemaking that have occurred in your life this week? Have you had a chance to bring a good end to a disagreement with someone? Has there been an opportunity to help other people come to a better understanding between themselves? How did you respond?

- Consider a conflict that is happening in the world today. Do you think the conflict is justified in light of this principle?

Applying all eight of these principles on a daily basis is a challenge. Over time, however, if you are consistent, they become second nature and will empower you to respond in an authentic, faith-filled way to situations you encounter.

Prayer

At the center of all Catholic social teaching are the transcendence of God and the dignity of the human person. The human person is the clearest reflection of God's presence in the world; all of the Church's work in pursuit of both justice and peace is designed to protect and promote the dignity of every person. For each person not only reflects God, but is the expression of God's creative work and the meaning of Christ's redemptive ministry.

(USCCB, *The Challenge of Peace*, number 15)

Close with this or another prayer:

God,

You have created us all to be like you. Help me to see my own value and the worth of every person I meet. Open my eyes to understand more deeply the ways the world breaks people's hearts and spirits. Thank you for the light you give us, showing us the path to a better world.

Amen.

Chapter 6
CHARITY OR JUSTICE?

Distinguishing Between Charity and Justice

Many who work generously to help people in need remind us of the importance of distinguishing between *charity* and *justice*. Charity and justice are two important but distinct responses to the people in need. Briefly, charity addresses people's immediate needs—it feeds people who are hungry, provides clothes to people who need them, gives shelter for the night to the homeless. One definition of *justice* is "right relationships." Work for justice attempts to change the underlying causes of homelessness and hunger and the lack of necessary resources.

> Charity will never be true charity unless it takes justice into account.
>
> (Pope Pius XI, *Divini Redemptoris*)
>
> Give a child a fish and he eats for a day; teach a child to fish and he eats for a lifetime.
>
> (Chinese proverb)

Justice is in one sense a deeper response to the problems around us. By way of comparison, imagine you come to school one day feeling really low. Your mother is battling cancer. Her struggle is putting stress on your family, and you feel as though you're getting lost in the shuffle. Your grades have been slipping, and you have a major social studies paper due that day. It's not done, and the teacher is strict. On top of that you forgot your lunch, and you don't have any money.

A friend notices you're missing lunch. He's a nice guy, so he shares his lunch with you. You start to talk about what's getting you down, but the conversation makes him uncomfortable and he clearly doesn't want to talk about it. He pats you on the back, wishes you a good day, and walks away.

You would be grateful for the lunch. But you would also feel as though a big part of you was invisible to the person whose back was heading away across the cafeteria. You might almost wish your friend hadn't even bothered to stop. Charity without justice is similar. It can turn a blind eye to the deeper problems so many people face in their everyday lives.

Charity

Much service work falls in the category of charity. The term *charity* can carry a number of meanings. Just look at the sidebar on this page to see some of the many meanings of the word *charity*.

charity. A theological virtue by which we love God above everything, and our neighbor as ourselves because of our love for God.

charity. A handout. May cause some people to answer, "I don't take charity." Charity can carry the connotation of, "I'm superior to you because I have more and you have less."

acts of charity. Actions to help other people. We generally think of performing acts of charity for people we don't know. We don't talk about performing acts of charity for family or friends.

charity. An expression of love in the form of helping people with their immediate needs.

We will use the last meaning of charity from the sidebar in this discussion. When we take up a collection for a sister parish in Central America, or serve a meal at a homeless shelter, or help at a Christmas party for lower-income children, we take care of an immediate need. We perform a very important service—but a service that will need repeating. Soon, perhaps tomorrow, our sister parish will be strapped for money; next week, a different team of volunteers will serve at the shelter; next Christmas those same children, or children very much like them, will need help to have a special Christmas.

The need for charity is pretty obvious. If we're willing to look, we can plainly see people in the world who desperately need our help. Sitting at the lunch table with nothing to eat is obvious—stress at home and a plummeting grade point average can remain hidden unless someone is willing to listen and go beneath the surface of a conversation.

Justice

Action for justice is different. Action for justice addresses the causes of poverty in Central America, or homelessness, or children whose families can't provide for them. Although it is essential that people be fed and clothed today, unless the underlying causes of poverty and injustice are addressed, the numbers of those in need will just continue to grow.

The need for justice is illustrated in this well-known story:

An extended family was picnicking on the bank of a river. They were having a wonderful time: the sun was shining, the children were playing, and hamburgers were cooking on the grill. Suddenly one of the children gave a shout. "There's a baby floating down the river!" Everyone ran to the shoreline, and sure enough, there was a baby struggling, helpless in the water. One of the adults immediately dove into the river, fought against the current, and managed to bring the infant to shore. Everyone immediately surrounded him, trying to comfort and warm the baby. In the midst of their efforts, another child piped up.

"There's another baby in the river!"

The group turned and gasped as they saw another terrified child swept along by the river. When they rushed to the shore and looked upstream, they could see more and more babies floating down the river. Several adults dove into the water, swimming valiantly to rescue the babies from the water.

Quietly, one of the adults began heading up the shoreline.

"Where are you going?" called a swimmer. "We need your help to get these babies to shore!"

"I'm going upstream," was the reply. "I've got to find out who is throwing all these babies in the river."

The story is not realistic, but it makes a point. Although it is very important to help people with their immediate needs, there are reasons why people find themselves without shelter or good shoes or school supplies. Justice is the hard work of trying to sort out the reasons why something is happening and then trying to do something about it. Work for justice is work to bring about relationships of respect and equality among all people and all groups of people.

The Two Feet

Charity and justice can be described as two feet used to journey through our world. Both are necessary and important. Just as you need both of your feet to walk comfortably and efficiently, so our world needs both charity and justice. If people refuse to work for charity, children would starve to death before justice efforts could benefit them. If people work only for charity, children of tomorrow will spend their days dependent on the generosity of others, generosity that may or may not arrive.

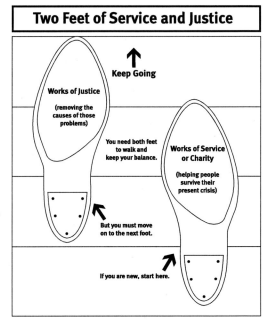

Two Feet of Service and Justice

Keep Going

Works of Justice
(removing the causes of those problems)

You need both feet to walk and keep your balance.

Works of Service or Charity
(helping people survive their present crisis)

But you must move on to the next foot.

If you are new, start here.

The Five Stages of Service

Although coming to see the difference between charity and justice is helpful, real life is more complicated. We can better understand our work if we see there are really five categories of service: taking up collections, direct service, service for empowerment, analysis, and advocacy.

What's the point of trying to put your service project into some kind of category? Because without some serious reflection, most of us would never move beyond charity. The need for charity is so much easier to see than the need for justice, and acts of charity are usually less complicated than action for justice. Sharing your lunch with someone can be a lot easier than really listening to them and trying to help them in a complicated situation.

If you think about it, almost every service project you can think of is most likely charity rather than justice. Most people who are involved in justice work started out doing charity. But the world needs, and God asks, that some people move into justice work. You might be one of the people called. Taking a look at other options can open our eyes to work that is important—and that we might enjoy and find fascinating.

Stage One: Taking Up Collections

Taking up a collection is among the simplest, most direct response to people in need. We collect money, food items, toiletries, or clothing, and distribute them to people nearby or in another country. Those collections provide immediate relief for people who are cold or hungry or sick. The downside is that often we don't have any contact with the people we are serving. But it's hard to make a mistake taking up a collection for someone.

People do make mistakes, however. Those errors arise from a limitation of many people's efforts: not really looking at and listening to the people we serve. For example, people in many other countries are smaller than the average North American. Sending extra-large men's pants or size 13 shoes to a sister parish in Nicaragua probably isn't going to help many people. You may have had the experience of feeling disappointed and even hurt when a family member gives you a gift that makes it clear they have no idea of who you are. In the same way, people opening boxes of items they cannot possibly use can be disappointed and hurt as well. Even something as straightforward as taking up a collection improves with information and careful listening. And learning about our world is one of the great benefits of doing service.

Stage Two: Direct Service

Many of our efforts take the form of direct service. Direct service involves going out into the community and helping someone ourselves. It might mean mowing lawns for the elderly, helping build a Habitat for Humanity house, sandbagging during a flood, or serving a meal at a soup kitchen. Most of these opportunities will give us some direct contact with the people we serve. We may find ourselves in new situations, some of which may make us uncomfortable. We get the opportunity to learn about a part of the world we did not know. Direct service often puts us in touch with people who touch our hearts and make us want to do more.

Like taking up a collection, direct service takes care of important needs. But it does not deal with the underlying causes that create those needs. It is charity rather than justice.

Stage Three: Service for Empowerment

Some of you may be involved in a perhaps more challenging form of service. Service for empowerment helps people begin to take more control over their own lives. Service for empowerment helps people gain new skills, knowledge, or experience, or develop personal qualities that improve the quality of their lives for a long time to come.

You are working toward empowerment when you tutor a second grader in math, help a new immigrant learn English as a second language, coach children in T-ball, or teach an elderly person computer skills. Long after you have left, the people you serve will have those skills at their disposal. They may also have learned a greater confidence in their own abilities. They probably feel more control over their lives, an extremely important ingredient in people's sense of security and happiness.

Most service projects fall under one of these three categories. Take a look around. Is your service project a collection effort? Is it direct service? Is it service for empowerment? How about the projects of others in your parish or school?

Resilience

As a teenager you have a unique ability to help children and younger teens. You are at a stage of life that many children look up to and idolize. Some of the children you work with may not have a stable person in their lives who looks out for them, who looks in their eyes and sees them as special and unique. You may know what those children feel like.

A great deal of study has been done on what is called *resilience*. We all know that two children growing up in the same difficult environment may move on to totally different lives. One will find success and love, whereas the other hits a downward spiral into addiction or other self-destructive behavior.

One factor emerges in virtually every study. Resilient children usually have one significant adult in their lives who cared about them, saw them as important, and helped them see they could have possibilities. The adult may have been a teacher, an aunt or uncle, a neighbor, a coach, or even a stranger. Many adults coming from difficult backgrounds look back and say, for example, "I realized that I could succeed in school when my third-grade teacher told me I was smart and showed me I could learn math." One caring person had the power to help a child turn the corner toward eventual happiness.

You have the opportunity to be that significant person in a child's life. As a teenager, your acceptance and affirmation may hold even more weight than an adult's. Think back to when you were in elementary school, and what you thought of "the big kids" around you. Children see you in the same light. Some things to keep in mind as an important person in a child's life:

- See the child for who he or she is and for who he or she can be.
- Keep your promises.
- Tell the truth.
- Let them know you like them and care about them.

Commitment

Take a few moments to reflect on who needs your affirmation right now. How can you empower that person or persons—of any age? Write a commitment describing how you can affirm those you encounter in your service work this week.

Stage Four: Analysis

The fourth stage, analysis, happens when we start to wonder why things are the way they are. You are driving to your service project, or you walk in the door, or you hear a comment or have a conversation. Suddenly it just hits you: "Things shouldn't be like this." Children shouldn't be living in homeless shelters. Or people with mental illness should not be left untreated and on the streets. Or the stream by my school shouldn't be polluted. Why are these things allowed to happen?

Teaching people empowering skills sticks a toe over the line into work for justice. Beginning to ask the question "Why?" moves one solid foot into justice territory. Analysis is asking those questions in a systematic way. It is being willing to do some digging, to ask for more information, and to look past answers that make no sense. Analysis of issues and situations is an essential part of Catholic social justice. We'll talk more about how to do analysis in the next two chapters.

Stage Five: Advocacy

Advocacy means standing up for someone else and working to bring about change in their circumstances. More specifically, it's about changing systems or institutions rather than individual circumstances.

For example, some who volunteer in nursing homes discover the care is not as good as it might be. Many nursing homes work with very limited budgets, and the staff is often overworked and underpaid. In addition, some individual staff members may not care about doing a good job, or some nursing facilities may have bad policies or practices. You might find yourself volunteering in a nursing home that overmedicates its residents to keep them more manageable and make life easier for staff.

If you were assigned to spend time with an individual resident and noticed a problem, you might alert the family and encourage them to ask for an adjustment in medication. This would be advocating for the patient, but it would not be advocating for justice. Taking on a justice challenge would mean working, by yourself or with others, to persuade the facility to change its policies. Advocacy often takes a different kind of courage than is found in direct service. Advocacy requires that we are willing to confront bad situations and deal with the resistance that may come when we speak up.

Many issues are bigger than any individual or agency. A nursing home may overmedicate its residents because their state funding was cut and they needed to reduce staff. A lake may be polluted because farmers and homeowners nearby use fertilizers excessively in spite of a community campaign to conserve. Some problems can be solved only by government action—and it is the job of concerned citizens to encourage government to take right action. You are a citizen, and you can become concerned.

Advocacy is unfamiliar to most people, and at first it can be intimidating. But as we will see, the church teaches us that as a community we need to take action targeted at the roots of our problems. The next few chapters will take a look at how that can happen.

Test Yourself

Theory doesn't do us much good until we're able to apply it to everyday life. As practice, decide whether the following scenarios are examples of which of the following:

C	taking up collections
DS	direct service
SE	service for empowerment
AN	analysis
ADV	advocacy

Some scenarios may have more than one answer.

____ An ecology class monitors water quality in a nearby stream and reports to their city council on their findings.

____ A student spearheads a fund-raising event to sponsor HIV/AIDS awareness in Africa.

____ A group of students call their legislators to request an increase in state funding for education.

___ A student teaches an elderly person to use a computer.

___ A group of concerned people perform a study to discover why a stretch of highway is the site of so many serious accidents.

___ A student accompanies a person with developmental disabilities to his or her bowling league.

___ A social studies class takes a spring day to clean up a stretch of highway.

___ A student volunteers at an animal shelter exercising dogs.

___ A community group organizes to limit the capacity of a nearby landfill.

___ A class studies the history of border conflict between Mexico and the United States.

Discovering Our Call

If you listen, you may notice debate between some people who promote efforts for charity and others who are strong on justice work. Some folks who work in justice seem to think that people who work in charity haven't quite grown up. Some people who work hard in charity efforts worry that justice people are rocking the boat or working on the wrong side of the political fence.

The truth is that both justice and charity are necessary. Jesus made it clear we are all called to be generous. Matthew leaves no doubt that Jesus expects us to take care of those in need.

> Then the righteous will answer him, "Lord, when was it that we saw you hungry and gave you food, or thirsty and gave you something to drink? And when was it that we saw you a stranger and welcomed you, or naked and gave you clothing? And when was it that we saw you sick or in prison and visited you?" And the king will answer them, "Truly I tell you, just as you did it to one of the least of these who are members of my family, you did it to me."
>
> (Matthew 25:37–40)

How we are to respond is an individual decision. God may be calling you to acts of charity at one point in your life and invite you to work for justice at another time in your life. The project you are working on now may open your eyes to a need you had not yet discovered.

In the next few chapters we will invite you to do some analysis, and give you some of the tools you need. Who knows where that path may lead you?

Prayer

> . . . And what does the Lord require of you
> but to do justice, and to love kindness,
> and to walk humbly with your God?
>
> (Micah 6:8)

Take some time alone, either outside in a quiet spot or perhaps in your bedroom. If you are inside, you might want to light a candle or put on some quiet music. Quiet yourself and set the day's worries aside.

Read the Scripture passage above, and take some time to reflect. Justice, kindness, and humility are the hallmarks of a person living according to Jesus's message. How do you show those qualities in your life? What are two areas where you could grow in these qualities?

Chapter 7
UNDERSTANDING WHAT YOU SEE

What Assumptions Do You Bring?

We said in the first chapter that service offers an opportunity to expand our view of the world and help us see people and events more clearly. We also talked about myths and assumptions—beliefs we carry that don't accurately represent the way the world works. Although you are almost certain to have new experiences in your service project, it is possible that what you see could simply reinforce some inaccurate assumptions you already hold. Without new information and time to reflect, service sometimes reinforces rather than transforms a view of the world that is limited by our own lack of information.

You may need new information to truly understand the people you meet. There is a good chance you are working with people who are different from you in some way: they are older or younger than you are, they may come from a different culture, they may have a different level of physical or mental ability. If you interpret their behavior simply from the framework of your own background and experience, you run the risk of misunderstanding their intentions and choices. In this chapter, we will look at some of the factors shaping individual choices and attitudes among the people we serve.

Assumptions That Can Get in the Way

We are often unaware of our assumptions. The following statements express assumptions that could affect how you handle yourself in your service work. Mark the following statements as true or false. Notice whether sometimes your reflex response differs from what you know to be true after you take time to think. Those responses are examples of ways you have already challenged some of your assumptions. Some statements are obviously false, and yet many people find themselves acting as if they were true. Some statements are a matter of opinion, but your opinion will influence your responses to the people and situations you encounter.

1. ____ People with disabilities should always be treated especially gently.
2. ____ When elderly people become physically fragile, they need others to make decisions for them.
3. ____ Children who live in poverty usually have trouble academically.
4. ____ If someone doesn't speak English very well, it helps if you talk louder.
5. ____ People in different cultures have varying standards for how to handle conflict.
6. ____ Women in abusive relationships should have enough self-respect to just get out.

The following pages explore some ideas that can help you better understand people you may encounter over the next weeks or months. We will look at the wide range of resources people need to cope with challenges, unspoken rules that govern the way people behave, learned helplessness, the impact of generations of poverty, and cultural differences.

Assets and Resources

In your work you might encounter people who seem to make choices that contribute to the pain in their lives. It may seem obvious to you that there are better ways of doing things, and the lives of the people you serve could be easier if they would make better choices. For example, you may observe people spending their limited money on items you consider frivolous under the circumstances. A group of young people on a mission trip to an Indian reservation wondered why they were painting houses when the unemployment rate on the reservation would seem to leave people with plenty of time to paint their own houses. On one level, that is a reasonable question. Understanding the answer requires some additional information.

Understanding Resources

People make choices for a reason. People sometimes make choices because they are compensating for losses in their lives that are invisible to us—unless we look closer. You have chosen to serve because there is a need. But needs go beyond lack of money or physical resources. We often take for granted the resources we have and the role they play in our decisions. For example, you may assume that everyone has family and friends who care for them. It may be hard for you to imagine the life of a young person who comes to the United States alone from another country, leaving behind family, friends, and community.

Dr. Ruby Payne has developed a list of resources that everyone needs in order to have a full life (see *A Framework for Understanding Poverty*, Highlands, TX: Aha! Process, Inc.,

1996). This list includes financial, emotional, mental, spiritual, physical resources, support systems, relationships or role models, and knowledge of hidden rules. We rely on all these resources to cope with the challenges in our lives. The fewer resources a person has, the more difficult it becomes to manage the ups and downs of life effectively.

The following is a brief description of each of these resources:

- Financial resources refer to the amount of money people have at their disposal to take care of their needs.
- Emotional resources refer to people's ability to handle their own emotions productively. People learn emotional responses from those around them; some people's ability to handle emotions is limited by chemical or structural damage to their brain.
- Mental resources are the ability to process information and use it effectively. Mental resources are affected by the quality of our education and experiences and by the development of our brain and nervous system.
- Spiritual resources are not necessarily church-related. Spiritual resources include a relationship with God or a power greater than ourselves. This relationship provides us with strength and guidance, and a sense that our lives have purpose and meaning even when we experience intense loss or other suffering.
- Physical resources refer to having full use of our bodies and the ability to live without disabling pain.
- Support systems refer to our ability to find help from other people when we need it. Families, churches, schools, friends, and neighbors can all be support systems. Our support systems may require us to give as well as receive support.
- Relationships or role models refer to the people in our lives who teach us how to behave and how to cope with difficulty. For children, the primary role models are parents or other caregivers. Coaches, teachers, neighbors, extended family members, and others can also be role models. You can be an important role model to someone you serve.
- Knowledge of hidden rules refers to the expectations various groups have of people who enter the group. For example, new students in a school, whether underclassmen or transfer students, need quickly to figure out the unspoken rules of the school, such as freshmen don't block the path of seniors in the school halls, in order to be successful.

Self-Assessment

You can have a more understanding and compassionate response to the people you're working with if you are aware of your own resources (and lack of them) as well as theirs. Take some time to reflect on the following questions. You do not need to share your answers with anyone.

- *Financial resources:* Do I know that my parents can take of important needs such as transportation, shelter, food, and clothing?

- *Emotional resources:* Have I learned how to cope with stress effectively? Do I deal with depression or anxiety? Can I handle conflict effectively?

- *Mental resources:* Have I received an adequate education? Do I have learning disabilities? Do I have a place where I can study and do homework? Do I have particular difficulties with certain subjects?

- *Spiritual resources:* Do I have a consistent sense of connection with God? Do I feel that I have an important place in the universe? Do I have people with whom I can share my spirituality?

- *Physical resources:* Am I able to move my body as I would like? Do I live with chronic pain? Can I get medical care when I need it? Do I have the full use of all my senses, especially sight and hearing?

- *Support systems:* Do I have family and friends who care about me? Are there people I can turn to when I need help? Do I have a sense of belonging in my community?

- *Relationships or role models:* Do I have people I look up to and who help me learn how to behave effectively as an adult?

- *Knowledge of hidden rules:* What groups do I belong to (family, friends, teams, school, ethnic group, gender, neighborhood, and so on)? Do I understand what is expected of me in each of those groups? Have I learned how to be successful in each of those groups?

Taking a Second Look

After you have answered the previous questions, take a look at the people you have met through your service project. Consider them as a group (the people who come into the homeless shelter, the kids who come to the after-school program) or choose one individual you have come to know. Using the same questions, what do you know or guess about their resources?

The purpose of this exercise is not to compare our life to other people's lives and decide which is better. We all have varying degrees of abundance and limitations in the resources described above. We often misjudge others' resources based on outside appearances. The purpose of this section is to better understand the challenges some people face. When we understand the limits of people's resources, we can have more compassion for them and the decisions they face. In addition, no one has all the resources in an ideal form. Taking a look at this list can also help us discover where we might want to build resources for ourselves.

- Do you see people make choices that could be a result of a lack of resources? How is the lack of one or more resources affecting their decisions?
- How might a lack of resources contribute to a woman's decision to stay in an abusive relationship?

Rules

Over time almost any group of people will develop hidden rules. Hidden rules are guidelines for behavior that everyone knows but rarely discusses. If you observe groups of friends at your school, you can see that different groups have different hidden rules. For example, some groups hug a lot and others don't. Some lend money without expecting to have it returned, while in other groups failure to return money would create a major problem. We often assume that other people do or should live by the rules we have grown up with. This assumption can trip us up when we move into a new environment.

If you are working in an environment that is new to you, you may find you are unsure about the rules of that group. You feel awkward because you are not sure what is expected of you. We are relieved if someone guides as we learn the rules and lets us know if we have broken a rule without realizing it.

You often learn these unspoken rules by seeing others break them or by breaking them yourself—and seeing the consequences. When you were very young, you learned what was considered acceptable in your school by watching who got picked on and why. You learned at a very young age just how important it was to obey unwritten rules.

People don't always obey the rules. For example, there are lots of rules about clothing. There is an unspoken understanding of which clothing styles fit which groups of people. If a middle-aged woman shows up wearing teenagers' clothes, everyone knows she has broken an important rule—but no one actually stops her from doing so.

People need to know what the rules are in order to follow them. Some people seem to have trouble picking up on hidden rules, and those people often struggle socially. Have you ever watched someone with poor social skills try to join a conversation? Social skills are the ability to recognize and navigate the rules of social interaction. Groups often quickly and effectively silence and exclude someone who is not playing by the accepted social rules.

Remember a time when you were with a new group of people and were not sure how to behave. This can happen in a service project, on entering a new school, visiting a friend's home for the first time, or in a new work situation.

- How did you feel? Did you accidentally break any rules? What important rules did you discover?

Rules and Economic Class

In our society, one set of rules has a very powerful impact on people's lives. These are the rules that pertain to economic class. Economic class is determined by the amount of money people have. *Middle class* refers to people who have what is considered an "average" amount of money, falling into the large space between the wealthy and those living in poverty.

It is not surprising that each of these three groups has hidden rules and that these rules differ. Dr. Payne in her book *A Framework for Understanding Poverty* (Highlands, TX: Aha! Process, Inc., 1996) notes that schools and workplaces generally abide by middle-class rules. In those settings, people are expected to speak standard English, be prompt and organized, and adults are expected to dress by middle-class standards. To be successful in most schools or workplaces, it is important to learn and abide by many of the rules of the middle class. This may not be fair, but it is how much of society functions.

In school or work settings, people may be considered less competent or acceptable when in fact they simply do not know or choose to disregard middle-class rules. For example, a person who interviews for a job in business may be passed over if she or he:

* dresses too casually or too flamboyantly
* speaks too loudly or too timidly
* brags about his or her achievements
* stands too close to people she or he meets

Those choices may have nothing to do with the requirements of the job. Unwritten, and sometimes unconscious, rules require that job applicants conform to certain expectations about fitting in. As a result, people may have difficulty breaking out of poverty if they do not have the opportunity to learn the rules of the middle class. They will be excluded from jobs and other opportunities that are important to achieving financial security.

This is not to say that middle-class rules are better. The point is to become more conscious of the rules we have learned and to be conscious of not making judgments about people simply because their rules are different from ours. Whenever we enter a new environment we discover valuable new ways of doing things, and we may discover rules that don't serve us well. Discovering more about the rules of a given group can help us understand people better and respond more effectively.

Learned Helplessness

Depending on where you serve, you may encounter a phenomenon called "learned helplessness." Chances are the people you serve have come up against some challenges. Some people, through no fault of their own, have been defeated by those challenges on a regular basis. Learned helplessness is the response some people develop when they have tried repeatedly to accomplish a goal and have not been able to succeed.

Years ago, social scientists conducted an experiment with dogs. The dogs were kept in cages with floor mats that could deliver an electric shock. During the experiment, the dogs were shocked at random intervals, without having any means of escape. At first the dogs scrambled frantically at the walls of their cages, but over time they gave up and simply lay on the mats. Eventually the doors to the cages were opened. The dogs had become so discouraged by their pain and defeat that they made no attempt to escape, even though there was no longer an obstacle to freedom.

Today, for good reason, such an experiment would not be allowed because of the suffering it caused. But the lesson learned is important. People living in painful circumstances, particularly when they have little control over unpredictable circumstances, can develop an attitude of defeat. This can happen to people living in poverty, abuse, or who have physical or mental disabilities. If you have ever been discouraged by trying to learn a subject that is difficult for you, or to participate in a sport or activity that is really not "your thing," you have a taste of how this feels.

It is easy to be critical of people who don't seem to try hard enough. Some people may be dealing with outside systems you don't understand; we will speak more of that in the next chapter. Some people may have been defeated in one situation and then transfer that attitude to another, like a student who has trouble with math and then gives up on school altogether.

Situational poverty describes people who become poor because of a divorce, job loss, or illness. People living in situational poverty often have resources to move back out of poverty. Situational poverty is not as powerful as generational poverty, when people who grow up poor had parents and perhaps grandparents who were poor as well. Generational poverty can bring about an especially powerful form of learned helplessness. People living in generational poverty often are surrounded by people who have known only poverty, who also have the repeated experience of trying to get control of their lives but are defeated for reasons they don't understand. People who experience such defeat may have lost hope of having long-term control over their lives, and so use their resources in ways that may help them cope with their circumstances but not change them.

How could this awareness help students understand why people living on an Indian reservation would not take good care of their houses?

• Do you see examples of learned helplessness among the people you are serving? Can you see examples in yourself or people in your everyday life?

Cultural Differences

Your service work may expose you to people whose cultures are different from your own. The *dominant culture* is a term sometimes used to describe white, middle-class culture. The dominant culture is the one most often represented on TV and in other media. Whatever your own cultural background, you have probably been exposed to the dominant culture through the media, school, or a workplace. People who come from the dominant culture, however, may not have much exposure to other cultures. We generally interpret other people's behavior based on our cultural assumptions. You may misunderstand people's behavior if they come from a background different from your own. A few examples of cultural differences are given in the following sidebar titled, "What Does It Mean?".

What Does It Mean?

Jumping up and down shouting, "We're number 1!"

Dominant culture | Other cultural understandings
Celebrating victory | Showing unacceptable competitiveness and individualism

Looking someone straight in the eye

Dominant culture | Other cultural understandings
Showing confidence and respect | Showing disrespect

Keeping eyes averted

Dominant culture | Other cultural understandings
Showing shame or dishonesty | Showing proper respect

Having blood drawn

Dominant culture | Other cultural understandings
Taking part in a reasonable medical procedure | Violating the spirit of a person

Talking back to a parent

Dominant culture | Other cultural understandings
Often considered acceptable | Showing disrespect

Talking back to a teacher

Dominant culture | Other cultural understandings
Disrespectful | Legitimate challenge of authority

Describing an incident, without emotion and in chronological order

Dominant culture | Other cultural understandings
Being reasonable and rational | Being boring

Placing your hand palm up, holding your fingers together and moving them toward you and away from you.

Dominant culture | Other cultural understandings
Beckoning someone closer | Saying good-bye

Using vulgar language in public

Middle class culture | Other cultural understandings
Unacceptable | Often accepted

Part of the fun of service, or of traveling to another country, can be learning about other cultures. When we encounter other cultures, we become more aware of our own. If you are working with people whose culture is different from your own, you have an opportunity to broaden your awareness of the world and the range of responses available to you.

Becoming aware of our own unexamined assumptions can help us understand the people we meet through service. Awareness can help us adjust more easily to new situations like college or work and be more successful in communicating with people we meet throughout our lives. This understanding is also a good first step toward investigating the structures and circumstances that support some of the inequalities in our society.

Prayer

Now there are varieties of gifts, but the same Spirit; and there are varieties of services, but the same Lord; and there are varieties of activities, but it is the same God who activates all of them in everyone. To each is given the manifestation of the Spirit for the common good. . . . All these are activated by one and the same Spirit, who allots to each one individually just as the Spirit chooses.

(1 Corinthians 12:4–7,11)

Close with this or another prayer:
Father,
You have created each of us in your image,
    and yet we are all so different.
You are with us in our similarities
    and in our uniqueness.
Please help me to recognize and value
    the dignity of each person I meet.
Bless me with an open heart
    so I can love as you have loved.
Amen.

Chapter 8
DIGGING DEEPER

The Other Side of the Coin

In chapter 6 you began the process of analysis—the process of asking the question "Why?" In that chapter we asked why some people who have less power and privilege make the choices they do. We examined the ways class rules, a lack of resources, and the impact of generational poverty and learned helplessness affect the choices people make. We looked at differences in cultural norms and how they can cause confusion as people interact with one another.

In this chapter, we will look at the other side of the coin. We will ask questions about those who do hold positions of power and privilege. We will begin to look more deeply at the systems and institutions that create and perpetuate unfair distribution of resources. We will take up some tools to examine more deeply the unseen forces that keep so many people in a position of powerlessness.

Asking the Question

Before we begin this work, let's go back to your experience in your service project. At the end of your day's work you go home. On the way you may catch yourself having some of these thoughts, "Boy, am I lucky. I don't . . ."

    . . . move every three months.
    . . . worry about violence in my home.
    . . . regularly eat dinner at a social service agency.
    . . . live with strangers.
    . . . have to speak an unfamiliar language every day.

Or you may think, "Boy, am I lucky. I do . . ."

    . . . have a body that works pretty well most of the time.
    . . . have a family who love and protect me.
    . . . have friends I can see regularly.
    . . . go to school where I can get a good education.
    . . . live in a neighborhood where I don't worry about violence.

On one hand, service reminds us to be grateful for the good things we have. We may have some of the challenges listed on page 76. Even so, through our projects we've probably met people whose difficulties are greater than or different from our own. They may have fewer resources than we do when it comes to money, family support, education, safety, good shelter, or health care.

Looking Long Term

Service often puts us in contact with inspiring people who meet incredible challenges with courage and a smile. We may find that in some ways the people we meet may have more joy in their lives than we see in our families and friends. Yet they live with serious hardships. And those hardships invite questions. The biggest question is, "Why?"

- "Why do so many little children spend the night in homeless shelters?"
- "Why do some public schools have beautiful buildings and the latest technology, whereas other schools in the same city have leaking roofs and a shortage of books?"
- "Why are so many people denied good health care?"
- "Why is our water polluted?"

These are important questions. Often we do not ask them until we have spent enough time in contact with people or in environments that invite us to look below the surface. As we said in chapter 6, simply taking care of the need at hand isn't enough. Twenty-five years ago homeless shelters sprang up across the country to address what people thought was a temporary need. The "temporary" need didn't go away—it got worse. It got worse for a reason, and until those reasons are addressed, the needs will continue to grow.

Many times when we get involved in service we find ourselves saying, "The world is not supposed to be like this." It's not. We can do something about it. You can do something that will make a lasting difference—a difference that will remain long after you've moved on to other ventures in your life. To do so, you need to be willing to do the work of digging deeper and discovering where lies the potential for long-term change.

Stories and Moments

Think back over your service experience or other times when you've been struck by injustice. What are some memories, some moments, that caused you to think, "This isn't right"? They might include the following:

- a child who flinches when he or she is touched
- an elderly woman who cannot afford her pain medication
- a polluted stream that cannot support life

List a few of your memories below:

1.

2.

3.

Stories and images are powerful. Many extraordinary leaders were inspired by a few memorable incidents in their lives. Stories and images motivate us, and when we tell stories we help other people understand our concerns and join us in our efforts.

In 1995, twelve-year-old Craig Kielburger read a newspaper story about a child laborer in Pakistan who was murdered for protesting the exploitation of children. Craig felt he needed to respond. His efforts became an organization called Free the Children, now active in thirty-five countries and involving over one million people in protecting children. Craig was forever changed by a story, and in turn his story has changed others.

Refer to the list of memories you just recorded and take a moment to write a more detailed description of one or two of these examples. Re-create the scene with as much detail as possible.

Some of the moments you recall were eased by your presence. A child taken from her or his family has your time and attention for a few hours. An elderly person has a freshly mowed lawn. A newcomer to our country learns some language skills.

Many of the moments that touch you invite a different type of response. Volunteering in an after-school program helps the children we meet, and some of those children will find new hope and confidence to carry on in their lives. But without a change in larger systems like education and health care, the numbers of children in need of help will continue to grow.

The Need to Analyze

Advocating for change in systems requires more thought and planning than does direct service. Systems are more complex than direct service, and well-meaning but uninformed attempts can actually do more harm than good. It's difficult to hurt someone while serving in a soup kitchen. Unless you spill hot soup on someone, providing a nourishing meal is usually uncomplicated and always a good thing to do. But changing a system without carefully analyzing the situation and the effect of our actions can waste energy or even sometimes hurt the people we intend to help.

For example, Minnesota has one of the largest Hmong populations in the country. The Hmong people lived in the mountains of Laos, and their lives were disrupted by the impact of the war in Vietnam. During the Vietnam conflict in the 1960s and 1970s, many of the Hmong people fought alongside the American forces. Many of those who came to the United States had lost family members to violence or starvation and had spent years in refugee camps. Many of the Hmong people who first arrived in Minneapolis began living in public housing units just outside the downtown area. These apartments were not particularly nice, but they were affordable.

An outside group decided that having such a high concentration of people of color living in one area constituted racism. They were successful in persuading the city to move people out of the housing project and scatter them around the metropolitan area.

Unfortunately, this group had not done a good job of consulting the Hmong community. Many people, particularly the older members of the community, did not want to move. They had already been uprooted from their homeland, lived in refugee camps, and then come to the United States. Even though their living situation had disadvantages, they had formed community with extended families and neighbors and did not want their lives disrupted once again.

As new immigrants, many members of the community could not speak English. They were unfamiliar with the way one advocates for change within the U.S. system of government. Many did not learn of the proposed change until it was too late to protest and would not have known what to do if they had been alerted earlier.

Older residents were moved to the suburbs without access to buses, were cut off from their community, their language, from grocery stores that sold familiar food. Their loneliness was intense and added to the incredible losses they suffered in Laos before coming to the United States. Several people vowed they would commit suicide if they were forced to leave. Well-meaning outsiders had come up with a solution that was not necessarily in the best interests of the community.

What appears to be an obvious solution still may not be the best solution. We need to investigate. Most important, we need to talk to the people who will be most affected by our actions. We need to have the courage and generosity to take a risk, to learn as much as possible, to pray for guidance, and then to do the best we can.

Asking the Right Questions

Your first awareness is that something is not right. Analysis moves us from simple concern to asking the right questions and then figuring out how to find the answers. Advocacy uses that information to bring about change. The next chapter will deal with bringing about change through advocacy. In this chapter we consider the questions to ask and some methods for finding answers. Some important questions are as follows:

- Why are conditions the way they are?
- What is the change I would like to see?
- Who has the power to make that change?
- How can I influence those people to bring about change?
- Who do I need to help me?

It really is that simple. And that complex.

For example, Stacy was volunteering in a nursing home. She was disturbed by the way some of the staff treated the residents. These staff members handled residents roughly, sometimes shouted at them, and ignored requests for help. When Stacy was able, she gently stepped in and took care of residents' needs, but she continued to worry about the impact of the staff's behavior. After several weeks of silently observing, she voiced her concerns to a supervisor.

The supervisor was aware of the problems and distressed by what she saw. But she informed Stacy that state funding had been cut to the residence, forcing the administration to cut salaries and staff. Because of the cuts, each staff member was responsible for caring for too many residents. And because of low salaries, the residence was unable to be as selective as they would like in hiring staff.

Analyze the above situation, using the following questions:

- Why are conditions the way they are?

- What is the change you would like to see in this situation?

- Who has the power to make the change?

At first glance, the problem appears to be a few unkind staff members and an inattentive supervisor. It would seem that asking the supervisor to hold the staff accountable would solve the problem. If Stacy had acted on what at first appeared obvious, she might have tried to get those staff members fired if they did not improve. But because her supervisor was willing to have an open conversation, Stacy discovered the problem was bigger than individual staff. Her answer to the third question will then determine her course of action. She may decide to advocate at the agency level— or she may decide to try to make a difference in state funding for health care.

Choosing the Scope: Institution or System?

When we take up a collection or engage in direct service, we benefit an individual or a group of people. We may help an agency deliver a service, but we do not change the agency itself.

When we ask questions about structural change, we begin to consider changing organizations or systems. Examples of individual organizations are schools, groups like the Sierra Club or the National Rifle Association, or nursing homes. Systems are more complex. According to the *Merriam-Webster's Dictionary*, a system is a form of social, economic, or political organization or practice, such as the capitalist system. We can examine systems such as the health care system, the educational system, the governmental system, the criminal justice system.

Accessible Space, Inc., is an organization started by Stephen Wiggins and Charles Berg while they were still in college. The summer after high-school graduation, Stephen's friend Michael "Hondo" Pesch was paralyzed in a swimming accident. Hondo went through a rehabilitation program in Minneapolis, but then had to return home to Austin, a small town in southern Minnesota. The only facility that could provide Hondo the care he needed was a nursing home.

These two young men could not stand to see their buddy's loneliness. With the help of supportive adults, they decided to find a way to build housing for their friend and other people who had suffered similar injuries. They researched government funding and managed to pull together over a million dollars to build their first five accessible housing units.

Over 1.1 million dollars. Two college juniors. Now, years later, Accessible Space, Inc., operates facilities in nine states. Their organization partners with a variety of institutions to make housing available and affordable to people with physical disabilities. Facilities are governed by their residents, who have an unusual level of control over how resources are used.

These two guys could simply have looked for a better living situation for Hondo. Instead, they examined the existing institutions and found them inadequate. Then they analyzed how to work with governmental and medical systems to create new options. They expanded their vision, then learned about federal and state funding, housing codes and restrictions, and the needs of people with disabilities. They listened to the residents, and they continue to do so. They worked with existing systems and created a new network of their own.

Choosing the Scope: Local, National, or International?

Charles and Stephen started their effort on a local level. Over time, their work has become national. Your answer to the question "Who has the power to make the change?" will determine whether you will work on a local, national, or international level.

For example, to get a stoplight put in at a dangerous intersection, you will probably work with the city. You would advocate for better funding for childcare programs at either the state or the federal level. If you are concerned about land mines or child labor, you could work at a national or international level. You may decide on the scope of your effort first, or the proper scope of your work may emerge after you start to do your research.

Doing the Research

Once you decide to bring about change on a deeper level than direct service, you may feel at sea. You may not know much about the government. You may not have any idea who to contact. Here are some tips for finding out more about your issue and how to help.

If at all possible, ask people directly involved. For example, if you learn that people you work with don't have adequate access to health care, ask them specifically what kinds of problems they experience because of lack of health care. If you know people knowledgeable about the issue, ask them for information as well. Specific information, and stories of people's struggles, will help you understand and spread the message. Write down what you learn, either as you speak with people or soon afterward. Documentation helps build your case.

Internet research. The Internet is an incredible source of information. Unfortunately, it carries a lot of misinformation as well. If you want to build your credibility as a resource on this issue, it's important you have your information straight. How can you tell if an Internet resource is reliable? It's hard to know for sure. But a few things to watch for are the following:

- Who's the source? Check the Web address. Is it a government agency? A commercial site selling something? An individual putting forth his or her ideas? A responsible publication?
- What's the slant? Watch the language used. Are there "loaded" words describing one side of the debate or the other? Does information seem to be presented fairly?
- How accurate is the information? Is it current or dated? Does the site indicate where the information was gathered? Are sources qualified professionals or activists in the field? How does the information match up with what you've already learned?
- Again—documenting your information is important. There's nothing more frustrating than having a great statistic supporting your position—and not being able to back it up.

Learning about government. You can gather an amazing amount of current information about the government on the Web. Many states have sites with profiles of your representatives, audio recordings of debates, and up-to-date information on bills and laws under consideration. You can get e-mail addresses of politicians and agencies affecting your concerns.

Books, newspapers, magazines, and the library. Your school or local library is a great source of information. Staff are usually happy to help you in your search. Your school librarian might turn out to be the best resource you could find. Don't be afraid to ask for help.

Once you get started, researching an issue can be fascinating. You may feel like a detective, and in many ways you are. You never know when you will turn up a critical piece of information, or when a lead will bring you to a whole new level of knowledge and awareness. Take yourself seriously. Knowledge is power, and you're in a position to gather a lot of persuasive information.

Once you've got information, it's time to decide on a strategy for bringing about change. Your research has revealed the causes of a problem. It's as if you've taken apart a computer and discovered why it was malfunctioning. The next step is to start putting the system back together in a new way that can better serve the purpose for which it was created.

Prayer

We have a song: "I have faith that all will change."
It must change if we truly believe
In the Word that saves
And place our trust in it.
For me, this is the greatest honor in the mission
The Lord has entrusted to me:
To be maintaining that hope
And that faith in God's people
And to tell them:
People of God, be worthy of that name.

(Archbishop Oscar Romero, "The Violence of Love sermon,"
September 2, 1979)

Close with this or another prayer:

Jesus,

You are the Word that came to teach us about a new way to live. Please help
us have faith in ourselves, in those we serve, and in the potential for change.
Help us to see all those we meet as our brothers and sisters. In particular help
us to see you in those who seem to stand in our way. Guide us in our study, as
we seek to discover the path to a better world.

Amen.

Chapter 9
ADVOCATING FOR CHANGE

Moving Past Analysis

Analysis is important, but by itself it will not make a difference in the world. Once we begin to understand some of the reasons behind poverty and injustice, we have the opportunity to work for change in the systems and institutions, keeping them alive.

You can be an advocate on your own, or you can join an already-existing effort. If the rights of prisoners are important to you, you can research the issue on your own, learn how to contact your legislators, and develop a publicity campaign. Or you can decide to start an Amnesty International group at your school and learn strategies that have already been used effectively in other communities.

Advocating for change involves answering the last of the questions posed in the previous chapter:

- Who has the power to bring about change?
- How can they be influenced to change?
- Who do I need to help me?

To Whom Should You Talk?

In chapter 8, you decided on the scope of your action. You decided whether you would try to make a difference at the level of an individual agency, your neighborhood, city, county, state, national, or on an international level. That decision tells you where to begin looking—it doesn't necessarily tell you who can bring about change. You need to try to discover who has the actual power to make a decision. Sometimes the person holding the power is the person with the highest position of authority: the governor, the president, the director of an organization. This is a good place to start. You may find, however, that other people hold the real ability to make a decision and bring about change.

For example, let's say you decide you want to advocate for better state funding for early childhood programs. You've learned the difficulties in the childcare agency where you work are the result of a cutback in outside funding to the agency. The governor is a good person to contact, as are your state senator and representative. But you may discover the people who hold the real power are the legislators who sit on a specific committee.

Attempting to bring about change by contacting the wrong people will result in disappointment. Perhaps you would like to set a new policy in your own school requiring athletic teams to buy their uniforms from companies that do not employ child laborers. It would seem the principal or athletic director would be the person to contact. In fact, you may need to make a presentation to your school board.

How do you find out who has the power for change? Ask and observe. Ask teachers, ask your political representatives, ask people working in the field. You may find out who has the power by making a proposal to the wrong people and discovering they don't have the power you need. False starts are part of the process. Anyone who gets involved in advocating for change runs into roadblocks. Don't be discouraged—just consider it part of the process and keep moving on to the next step. It's easy to feel you're in over your head, that you're trying to change something you don't really understand and haven't seen before. Take your work as a challenge, like solving a puzzle. Once you learn how to bring about change, you'll find yourself doing it again—for your own benefit or that of others.

The Story of San Lucas Toliman

People spend a lot of time trying to influence other people to change. Sometimes the most efficient response is simply to take matters into our own hands. An example is the mission of San Lucas Toliman in Guatemala.

Many years ago Fr. Greg Schaffer began working at the mission parish of San Lucas Toliman in Guatemala. He went to serve the spiritual needs of the people; he was struck by their physical suffering as well. Over the years he has developed a variety of medical, agricultural, and spiritual programs for the people of San Lucas.

One reason for poverty in San Lucas was the poor price farmers received for their coffee. Father Greg began a farmers' cooperative, much like cooperatives formed by farmers

Dealing with Power

Some people will caution, "But you're getting political!" or you may encounter people who think teenagers are too young to get involved in politics. Students at Jackson Elementary School in Salt Lake City, Utah, have cleaned up a hazardous waste site, gotten new laws passed, planted hundreds of trees, improved sidewalks, and secured grant money for a telephone hotline for abused children. Even children can work effectively with a political system.

Politics means handling power. Power is simply the capacity to make something happen. It can be handled badly, but in itself it is neither good nor bad. We deal with power every day—in relationships at home, at school, on the playing field, at work. When we do nothing to challenge the status quo, we are still being political—we are helping to maintain the current balance of power. When we take action, we can create a shift in the balance of power that will bring about a safer and more just society.

A power analysis is looking at who has the power in a given situation, how they got the power, and how they are holding on to that power. For example, older siblings may have power over you. They got the power when you were little and they were bigger and more experienced than you were. As you get older and more experienced, those power dynamics shift. Do they still have the same kind of power over you as when you were little? Just as growing older shifted the dynamics, working for systemic change means being more deliberate about discovering the sources of power and the means for change.

How Can People Be Persuaded to Change?

Once you've decided who you want to influence, how do you get your message across? Obvious first steps are phone calls, visits, e-mail and letter writing. Let people know you, your concerns, and what you would like to see changed. These methods work whether you're contacting the President of the United States or the president of your school board.

A few tips include these:

- Figure out precisely what you want to say and write it down. If you're making a phone call, use notes.
- Identify yourself. In particular, let the recipient know if you are a stakeholder—a current or future voter, living in their district, a student in the school, etc.
- Address the recipient correctly. Find out his or her current title and use it appropriately.
- Be concise. Make a point, support it with accurate information, and sign off.
- Offer to follow up and help.
- Be polite. Assume the recipient has good intentions and is willing to listen. Express any disagreement respectfully.
- Thank the recipient for listening and considering your request.

- Remember to contact those on the opposite side as well as those who are sympathetic to your cause.
- Write letters. You can write to the people in power as a way to convey your message. Also, don't forget about letters to the editor. Newspapers are a great—and free—way to get public attention for your issue. Be sure to be concise and avoid rambling; make every word count.
- Be persistent. Once may not be enough.

Specific Actions

So how exactly do you get heard? There are a variety of methods. You can speak to groups such as your parish, a class at school, your city council. You can write a proposal, get out the vote, and gather information by surveying or interviewing people. You can become a member of a board or council. And, if all else fails, you can consider protesting an issue.

Public Speaking

Follow the same guidelines as in writing: do your homework, stick to the topic, clearly state your request. Have a clear introduction, explanation, and conclusion. The best single piece of advice for keeping yourself calm is to concentrate on your topic rather than on yourself. People can tell if you care about your subject. Speaking to an audience gives you a chance to touch their hearts.

Proposals

Proposals can be a valuable way to get your message across. A proposal is a written statement outlining your requested change, describing the process and reasons for the change. The advantage of a proposal is that
- it's specific
- it's in black and white

Writing a solid proposal requires that you be concrete in your request and clear in your justification. It gives you documentation of your request, a source people can go back to if their memory fades. Negotiations often get bogged down because people get sidetracked and confused about the issue at stake.

People are often much more willing to respond to a specific request than a general desire for change. "We are requesting a new slide and a new surface for the playground," is much easier to respond to than, "We want a safer place for children to play." Putting time into developing a solid proposal can be well worth the trouble.

Raising Awareness

Campaigning, recruiting voters, and voting yourself are great vehicles for change that only present themselves every couple of years. Unless your project happens at election time, you may not able to get your point across in this way. If you really care about the issue, watch for an opportunity when the next election comes around. Research you do now will prepare you for action then.

Surveys and interviews can help you learn the lay of the land and also give you better information on your topic. They publicize your concern and may give you an opportunity to meet people who will help you. Write down the results of your work. Be able to cite your information specifically when using it later.

Moving into a Power Position

Getting yourself in positions of influence may be easier than you think. Teens often think they have no power—when in fact lots of avenues to power may be available to you. For example, your school board may have positions available for student advisors. Or they may be willing to add positions if you ask. The same goes for your city council. Adults in these positions are often impressed that young people are interested.

If a board or teen advisor position does not exist, you might want to start one. Suggest a teen advisory council—to your mayor, your school principal, a local environmental agency. Make your voice heard and invite others to share their voice on the topic.

Protesting

Protesting can be an effective way to be heard, but is best used only after previous methods have failed. Before deciding on a protest, be sure you've tried several of the previous actions mentioned. Usually it's not fair—or helpful—to protest without first giving the other side an opportunity to respond to your request. Protests tend to generate a sense of two opposing sides. Although people may have very different viewpoints, working with people rather than against them can be your most effective path whenever possible.

Protests include strategies such as marches, boycotts, or picketing. They work by drawing dramatic attention to an issue, and putting the opposition on the spot in such a way as to pressure them into responding. Protests can be effective, but they increase risks and investment. They should be considered carefully.

Remember to stay respectful when you're protesting, whether you're carrying signs or making speeches. Protests are a good time to remember, "What would Jesus do?" Don't let yourself get caught up in a negative contest. From a Christian perspective, we want to remember that our opponents are children of God. From a practical perspective, chances are they've got some power or you wouldn't be bothering to protest. Unless you can muster a lot of your own power, your best bet is asking them to share rather than trying to intimidate them into handing it over. Put yourself in their shoes.

Who Do You Need to Help You?

Going at an issue alone can be confusing and discouraging. An adult mentor can provide invaluable guidance and support for you. A teacher, youth minister, parent, or other experienced activist can help you develop strategies and avoid mistakes.

Joining forces with others improves your chances of being heard. Many voices create more volume than just one. You can start your own group. Call a meeting, publicize your purpose, and recruit people individually. Don't be shy. Even people who don't like drawing attention to themselves can learn to make noise for a cause they believe in. Talk to people and invite them to join your group. Person-to-person contacts are one of the most effective ways to build support. But there are other ways as well. Put up posters. Make announcements at school, if you can. Advertise in your parish. Write a press release for your local newspaper (yes, you can). Learn to tell your story. Naming your group can catch people's attention and make your focus clear. "Students Against Drunk Driving" is easy to remember and clearly lets people know the purpose of the group.

You can also link with existing groups. A larger effort provides you with support and direction, letting you put all your energy into working directly for change. Free the Children, founded by twelve-year-old Craig Kielburger, is now one-hundred-thousand strong. Together, these young people have made a profound difference across the world. Ask around, or check the Internet to see whether a group is already tackling a cause that is dear to your heart.

Look for adult support. Remember the story of Accessible Space, Inc.? Those young men found adults to support them, to give them advice and credibility as they tackled an enormous project. You can find support from adults while still maintaining your own leadership. Young people can do incredible things. You can be one of the people making change.

Finding Financial Support

Your efforts may require money to be successful, and you may not be able to provide much financial support yourself, so you may need to seek additional financial help. Some professional fund-raisers describe their work as "teaching people to be generous." Many people would say asking for money is even scarier than public speaking. When you solicit money for a good cause, you truly are giving people the opportunity to become more generous. As you've learned in your work, generosity brings its own rewards.

Before asking anyone to support you financially, be sure you have a sound plan for how the money will be used. You have a better chance of getting funds if you can explain briefly and clearly what you will do with it. You also have a responsibility to use people's donations wisely.

How Can You Raise Money?

Taking up a collection from your friends, classmates, or other contacts is a good start. You can sell goods or services: sell baked goods, pizza, or ice cream at your school, host a car wash, have a group of students baby-sit for families, putting all proceeds toward your cause. When raising funds, it is always important to think of every aspect of your fund-raiser. For example, if you sell food items during lunch at your school, be sure to obtain permission from the school administration and notify the kitchen ahead of time so they can adjust their food preparation.

Businesses can be great resources for financial support. Many are extremely generous with their goods and services or contributions of money. Again, it is important to be well organized, have specific purposes for the item(s) requested, and be respectful when approaching a business requesting a donation. Grant money may be available for your project. Grants are larger donations given by foundations and other organizations. Some parishes distribute grants to worthy causes. To receive a grant, you probably need to align yourself officially with a group. Foundations rarely give money to individuals. But some students have secured hundreds and even thousands of dollars for their programs.

Remember to keep records of the money you receive and spend. If you decide to apply for a grant the following year, they will expect a solid report on your previous spending. And keeping records is a way of showing respect for the investment you have received.

Advocating for change tends to carry a lot more surprises than direct service. You may find obstacles you hadn't expected; you may find successes beyond your wildest dreams. You will learn a lot in the process. Regardless of the outcome on a practical level, you will know you tried to make a long-lasting difference. You have done a little bit to bring the Reign of God into today's world.

Prayer

Where is faith capable of moving mountains?
Isn't it even harder to transform structures?
To transform structures will demand
the direct intervention of Christ himself
who at the same time will transform hearts and minds.

(Dom Helder Camara, August 28, 1971)

Close with this or another prayer:

Jesus,

The problems of the world are so great, and I am just one voice. You have promised that with faith we can do anything. Help me trust in you when I get discouraged. Guide me when the way seems blocked.

Give us the strength to move the mountains of injustice that block the way of peace. Thank you for coming into the world and sharing our struggles. Help us learn from your example.

Amen.

Chapter 10
EVALUATING AND CELEBRATING

How Is It Going?

It's time to stop and take stock of yourself and your work. Evaluation and reflection help us get the most out of what we are doing and to contribute as much as we possibly can. Too often, we leave at the end of the day, puzzling over some challenge. A child in our program is terribly shy, and it's not possible to draw him or her into activities. Another child is aggressive, and we're not sure how to handle him or her. But we get home, things get busy, and we come back the next week without any new ideas for a solution. It is too easy, after we've finished our project, to look back and think, "You know, I should have . . ."

Midterm Evaluations

Evaluation is valuable in the middle of a service project, and again at the end. Remember, evaluation does not mean looking only at the negatives—it includes naming the positives as well. Midterm evaluations help us make changes to improve our current project. This is a good time to reflect on the relationships you are developing, whether they are enjoyable or challenging. You can sort out your thoughts about an agency where you are working, or specific situations that are troubling. Reflection can help you recognize the ways you have already changed, and the effect those changes can have on your life away from your service project. An outside perspective can be invaluable here. Ask your supervisor, your parents, and the people you are serving for their advice and feedback. Their guidance and reassurance can give you a boost and help you do an even better job.

If You're Serving in an Established Project

Most students work with an established project, such as an after-school program for children, a nursing home, or an agency serving people with developmental disabilities. These questions can begin your reflection. You may have others as well.

1. Do you have a clear sense of your goals and responsibilities in relation to your role at the agency where you volunteer? Jot down the most important ones.

2. How would you describe your relationships with the people you are serving? other volunteers? your supervisor? Is there something you can do to improve these relationships?

3. How would you rate your success in your work? How are your skills improving? Which of your skills have been useful in your service experience? Where do you need to develop or sharpen your skills?

4. What had you hoped to accomplish? Are you on the road to making that happen? What might you do differently?

5. Who might help you accomplish your goals more effectively? What could you gain by asking for help?

6. Have you seen God in the people you've met? If so, describe when this happened. Has your faith changed or been challenged as a result of your experience? If so, how?

If You Designed Your Own Project

Evaluation is especially helpful if you designed your own project. Your plan is likely to change as you go along, and taking time to do some structured reflection will guide you toward a more effective strategy. In addition to the above questions, you can ask yourself:

1. What was my original plan? Is it working?

2. If it is not working as planned, do I need to keep on trying, or should I change strategies? If I need to change, what might be a more effective plan?

3. What new information have I gained that can help me come up with a good plan? What new information do I need to find?

4. What resources do I need and don't yet have? Who can help me get those resources?

If You're Doing Advocacy

Advocacy, which we described in chapter 9, is one of the toughest assignments you can take. If you joined an established advocacy effort, you have probably had people who helped you learn the ropes. If you had the courage to take on an issue independently, you have probably learned from trial and error. Use the following questions to begin evaluating your advocacy efforts.

1. Were you able to connect with the people who have the power to bring about change? Why or why not? Did they listen? Have they taken action?

2. How have your efforts made a difference?
    (Remember, advocacy can be slow and discouraging, and sometimes the results don't show up until much later. For example, a bill you support may be defeated this time around, but perhaps the work you and other people do will make a difference the next time the issue comes up for a vote.)

3. Do you need a new strategy to accomplish your goals? Why or why not? If yes, what is it?
    (Remember, even if you have to change your strategy, your time has not been wasted. You have gained new information on the process you could not have found another way.)

When You're Finished

A final evaluation is useful at the end of your project. Final evaluation helps us maximize the wisdom we take away from our service experiences. Evaluation can also help us share our new knowledge with others. You can use the questions from the previous pages, looking over the entire scope of your work. Were you able to make improvements after your midterm evaluation? Have there been any surprises since then?

   In addition to revisiting your midterm evaluation, you may choose to use the following questions for your final evaluation of your service experience. Remember to be honest and fair in your evaluation of yourself and where you volunteered.

1. On page 13, in chapter 1 of this book, you picked three areas in which you would like to grow as a result of your service work. Has that growth taken place? How?

2. What do you know now about yourself that you did not know before? What do you know now about the issue you were addressing through your service that you did not know before?

3. What is one challenge you handled particularly well? What is one area in which you struggled?

4. What would you like to learn more about, such as the issue of homelessness, the lives of children with disabilities, the political process?

5. How do you see life differently now?

6. On page 16, in chapter 1, you wrote about the expectations you had for yourself when starting your project. What are your answers now to the questions you asked?

Agency Evaluation

Evaluating the agency where you served is valuable for a number of reasons. If you had difficulty with your project, evaluating the agency as well as yourself may help you discover what went wrong. Challenging assignments can be great learning experiences, but not necessarily ones we want to repeat.

The next time you look for an opportunity, you will have a better idea of what you want and need. If you had a positive experience with an agency, reflection can help you be more aware of what you are looking for in terms of support and structure. If your experience was negative, evaluation can help you be more alert on what to avoid.

Although not all agencies are open to hearing it, they can benefit from feedback. We said earlier that most service agencies run on tight budgets and may have inexperienced volunteer coordinators or none at all. Your feedback can help them better retain volunteers in the future or can help new staff be more successful in their jobs.

If you have a service coordinator, your evaluation can be very helpful to him or her. The service coordinator may be able to give feedback to the agency that would be uncomfortable for you. Someone running a service program wants to develop strong relationships with agencies that support volunteers. Your honest evaluation can help you supervisor steer future volunteers into the best opportunities for them.

1. Was the intake process efficient? Did the agency return my calls?

2. Were my responsibilities clear?

3. Was someone available to answer my questions?

4. Did I get help if I had challenges? What type of help was offered?

5. Did I feel safe? Was I given adequate support in keeping myself safe?

6. Could I see other opportunities for service at the agency that weren't being developed? If so, what were they?

7. Were my hours documented accurately?

8. If I were in charge, what would I do differently? What would I do the same?

9. Would I recommend the agency to another volunteer? Why or why not?

10. What advice would I give to someone intending to volunteer at this agency?

Give a copy of your reflection to your service coordinator, if you have one. You may also want to share your reflection with the agency.

Celebrating

Service is hard work. You kept your commitment and invested yourself in your work. You have made new relationships, experienced an unfamiliar world, and contributed to other people's lives. That's cause for celebration. We celebrate beginnings and endings in many areas of our lives: graduations, Baptisms, end-of-season banquets, and the close of the school year. Your service work deserves a celebration, too.

You can celebrate with your class or Confirmation group. You can celebrate with the people you served. You can celebrate on your own or with friends and family. Think of what you most want to honor: new relationships, new skills, and the new parts of yourself you've discovered.

Celebrations can happen as you say good-bye, or at some point during your project. You might want to serve a traditional Thanksgiving dinner to a group of Somali children, or take some adults with developmental disabilities to the county fair. Have some fun—you deserve it. Be mindful that the people you are serving may decide to have a celebration for you. Make a special effort not to miss your final sessions so you don't accidentally disappoint them.

Saying Good-bye

Good-byes are special moments that will not come again. It is hoped that you have developed some important relationships during your project. Your memories of this time will be sweeter if you make the effort to say good-bye, particularly if you've been working with people to whom you mean a great deal. Children, the elderly, and people living in a facility may have developed very strong attachments to you. It will be easier for them to let go if you take the time to truly say good-bye. Many people are uncomfortable with good-byes. They feel awkward and perhaps don't know how to deal with the sadness or gratitude that may be expressed. Good-byes are a part of life, and learning to say good-bye graciously is a gift to yourself and others.

Saying good-bye includes saying thank-you. You deserve thanks for the work you've done, but chances are there are also people who have been generous with you. A mentor or supervisor has watched over you. The people you have served have shared themselves with you. Children may have hugged you. A weary elderly woman may have opened her heart and shared stories of her childhood. A longtime volunteer may have taken time out to show you the ropes.

Take time to say thank-you and good-bye. You are honoring people's openness to you and developing an attitude of gratitude. Gratitude is a key to happiness—one of the important lessons you may have observed in your work.

Telling Your Story

During your project you may have come to know a portion of the world in a new way. Of course, you knew there were elderly people in our society, and you knew that many of them were in nursing homes. But perhaps you did not know daily life in a nursing home. Perhaps you did not understand that so many of today's homeless are women and children. Perhaps you did not know what it was like to be an economically poor child, moving so frequently that keeping up in school is practically impossible.

"Social ministry must be done, for we cannot lose that part of our identity without losing what we as the people of God are called to be. May God, who has begun this good work in us, bring it to completion. And the people of God said, 'Amen!'"

(Reverend Larry Snyder, "Homily")

So many people are invisible in our society. So many people do not have the opportunity to make their voice heard. So many pressing issues go unnoticed. You can help make the people you have met and their concerns visible. You can help tell the story, but how? By speaking in conversation with other people and in more formal settings you can share your experiences. You can tell other students at your school about your experience. Perhaps you have discovered a gift in public speaking and you can share the story with civic groups or at your parish.

You can write to your local or school newspaper or to your legislators. You can tell the story in art or photographs. You can write a play. You can interpret and capture your experience for yourself and for others who can also make a difference. You have the power to keep the ripples expanding in the pool.

What Next?

Many students continue with their projects after their initial commitment is over. Perhaps you want to take a break. Other opportunities will present themselves in future years. Remember to consider them generously as time goes on. So often when we learn a big life lesson we think, "I am never going to forget this." And then we do.

* What do you most want to remember? whose face? what moments? what lessons?

* Would you like to make a promise—to yourself, to the people you served, to the future?

Prayer

Today you have come together to declare that in the new century you will not let yourselves be made into tools of violence and destruction; you will defend peace, paying the price in your person if need be. You will not resign your-selves to a world where other human beings die of hunger, remain illiterate and have no work. You will defend life at every moment of its development; you will strive with all your strength to make this earth ever more livable for all people.

Dear young people of the century now beginning, in saying "yes" to Christ, you say "yes" to all your noblest ideals. I pray that he will reign in your hearts and in all of humanity in the new century and the new millennium. Have no fear of entrusting yourselves to him! He will guide you; he will grant you the strength to follow him every day and in every situation.

(Pope John Paul II, World Youth Day address, August 19, 2000)

Close with this or another prayer:

> Jesus,
>
> You have promised to be with us wherever we may go. Help me to always follow you with a generous heart. Let me never forget your vision for our world and the role you ask me to play in it. Thank you for memories and insights I have gained. Please give me the grace to remember your message and live it every day of my life.
>
> Amen.

Acknowledgments

The scriptural quotations contained herein are from the New Revised Standard Version of the Bible, Catholic Edition. Copyright © 1993 and 1989 by the Division of Christian Education of the National Council of the Churches of Christ in the United States of America. All rights reserved.

The quotation on page 11 is from the January 26, 1999 address of John Paul II, "To the Young People at the Kiel Center," Saint Louis, Missouri, at *www.vatican.va/ holy_father/john_paul_ii/travels/documents/hf_jp-ii_spe_26011999_stlouis-arrival_en.html,* accessed August 30, 2005.

The prayer by Mother Teresa on pages 32–33 is from the "National Prayer Breakfast," February 4, 1994, found at the Minneapolis Television Network Web site, *www.mtn.org/tccg/documents/mt_addr.html,* accessed August 30, 2005.

The quotation by Margaret Mead on page 38 is from the Institute for Intercultural Studies Web site, *www.interculturalstudies.org,* accessed August 30, 2005.

The quotation by Peter Maurin on page 47 is from *Easy Essays,* by Peter Maurin (New York: Sheed and Ward, 1936). Copyright © 1936 by Sheed and Ward.

The list of principles on Catholic social thought on page 48 is from *Sharing Catholic Social Teaching: Challenges and Directions,* by the United States Conference of Catholic Bishops (USCCB), at *www.nccbuscc.org/sdwp/projects/socialteaching/socialteaching.htm,* accessed August 30, 2005.

The Special Olympics athlete oath on page 48 is from the Special Olympics Public Web site, *www.specialolympics.org/Special+Olympics+Public+Website/default.htm,* accessed August 30, 2005.

The list of "Catholic Social Teaching Principles" and "Common North American Cultural Attitudes" on pages 49–50 are adapted from *Journey to Justice: Transforming Hearts and Schools with Catholic Social Teaching,* by Constance Fourré (Washington DC: NCEA, 2003), page 6. Copyright © 2003 by NCEA. Used with permission.

The excerpt on page 57 is from *The Challenge of Peace: God's Promise and Our Response,* number 15, on the Office of Social Justice Web site, *www.osjspm.org/cst/cp.htm,* accessed August 30, 2005.

The quotation by Pope Pius XI on page 58 is from *"Divini Redemptoris,* Encyclical of Pope Pius XI on Atheistic Communism to the Patriarchs, Primates, Archbishops, Bishops, and other Ordinaries in Peace and Communion with the Apostolic See," at *www.vatican.va/holy_father/pius_xi/encyclicals/documents/hf_p-xi_enc_19031937_ divini-redemptoris_en.html,* accessed August 30, 2005.

The image of the "Two Feet" on page 60 is adapted from *Poverty and Faith Justice: An Adult Education Program on Christian Discipleship in the United States* (Washington DC: USCCB, 1998), page 20. Copyright © 1998 by USCCB, Inc. Used with permission.